MARKETING

BUSINESS 2000

James L. Burrow

SOUTH-WESTERN

TM

THOMSON LEARNING

Australia • Canada • Mexico • Singapore • Spain • United Kingdom • United States

SOUTH-WESTERN
™
THOMSON LEARNING

Business 2000
Marketing
by James L. Burrow

Vice President/Executive Publisher
Dave Shaut

Team Leader
Karen Schmohe

Executive Editor
Eve Lewis

Project Manager
Enid Nagel

Production Manager
Patricia Matthews Boies

Editor
Colleen A. Farmer

Executive Marketing Manager
Carol Volz

Channel Manager
Nancy A. Long

Marketing Coordinator
Yvonne Patton-Beard

Manufacturing Coordinator
Kevin L. Kluck

Art and Design Coordinator
Tippy McIntosh

Cover and Internal Design
Bill Spencer

Editorial Assistant
Stephanie L. White

Production Assistant
Nancy Stamper

Compositor
New England Typographic Service

Printer
Courier, Kendallville

About the Author
James L. Burrow, Ph.D., is the coordinator of the graduate Training and Development Program at North Carolina State University in Raleigh, North Carolina. He has been a faculty member at the community college and university levels in marketing and human resources development as well as a consultant to business and public organizations.

For permission to use material from this text or product, contact us by

Tel: 800-730-2214
Fax: 800-730-2215
Web: www.thomsonrights.com

For more information, contact South-Western, 5191 Natorp Boulevard, Mason, OH, 45040. Or you can visit our Internet site at

www.swep.com.

International Divisions List

Asia (including India)
Thomson Learning
60 Albert Street, #15-01
Albert Complex
Singapore 189969
Tel 65 336-6411
Fax 65 336-7411

Australia/New Zealand
Nelson
102 Dobbs Street
South Melbourne
Victoria 3205
Australia
Tel 61 (0)3 9685-4111
Fax 61 (0)3 9685-4199

Canada
Nelson
1120 Birchmount Road
Toronto, Ontario
Canada M1K 5G4
Tel (416) 752-9100
Fax (416) 752-8102

Latin America
Thomson Learning
Seneca 53
Colonia Polanco
11560 Mexico, D.F. Mexico
Tel (525) 281-2906
Fax (525) 281-2656

Spain (including Portugal)
Paraninfo
Calle Magallanes 25
28015 Madrid
Espana
Tel 34 (0)91 446-3350
Fax 34 (0)91 445-6218

UK/Europe/Middle East/Africa
Thomson Learning
Berkshire House
168-173 High Holborn
London WC 1V 7AA
United Kingdom
Tel 44 (0)20 497-1422
Fax 44 (0)20 497-1426

HOW TO USE THIS BOOK
ENGAGE STUDENT INTEREST

CAREERS IN MARKETING
Highlights a real-world company and the careers it offers to demonstrate various career possibilities.

LESSONS
Make the text easy to use in all classroom environments.

VIDEO
Contains clips from several resources that can be used to introduce concepts in each chapter.

The Chapter 3 video for this module introduces the concepts in this chapter.

PROJECT
Group or individual activity that has activities for each lesson.

CAREERS IN MARKETING

SPRINT CORPORATION

The Brown Telephone Company was formed in 1899 to provide local telephone service to communities in Kansas. It became Sprint Corporation in 1992. Over the years, the company has focused on being a technology leader. Sprint was a pioneer in the use of fiber-optic cable and digital switches.

Sprint's Asia Business Development Manager is responsible for product expansion in assigned countries. The manager gathers competitive intelligence, checks the economic, technological, and operational feasibility of ideas, and develops partnership relationships with other businesses.

The Manager needs a college degree in business, management, or engineering and five years' experience in the telecommunications industry. Financial and business analysis skills are essential as well as leadership, entrepreneurial, and negotiation skills. The manager needs to be fluent in English and the languages of the assigned countries.

THINK CRITICALLY
1. How do you think Sprint has been able to maintain its success?
2. What would you find interesting and challenging about the position of Business Development Manager?

CHAPTER 3

PLAN PRODUCTS AND SERVICES

LESSONS

3.1 THE PRODUCT

3.2 PRODUCT PLANNING

3.3 PRODUCT LIFE CYCLES

3.4 EFFECTIVE SERVICES

PROJECT
Develop Products

PROJECT OBJECTIVES
- Identify how customer needs influence product development
- Describe sources of new product ideas
- Analyze a new product to determine factors influencing its success
- Identify ways to provide effective services

GETTING STARTED
Read through the Project Process below. Make a list of materials and information you will need. Decide how you will get the needed materials or information.

PROJECT PROCESS

Part 1 **LESSON 3.1** Work in small groups to develop a questionnaire. The purpose of the questionnaire is to obtain feedback from customers on a company's products. Prepare at least 10 questions that help to determine what the customer likes and dislikes about the product, how it compares to other products, and what improvements they would like to see.

Part 2 **LESSON 3.2** In your groups, brainstorm ideas for improvements to existing products. Then brainstorm ideas for brand new products. After you complete the lists, share them with the other groups in your class. As a class, use a ranking procedure to identify the five product improvement ideas and five new product ideas you think have the greatest chance for success.

Part 3 **LESSON 3.3** Use the Internet to identify a new consumer product that has been introduced within the past two years. List two competitive brands for the new product. List the similarities and differences among the three brands. Identify advantages you think the new product offers to consumers compared to existing brands.

Part 4 **LESSON 3.4** Identify a service provided by a business in your community that you think is provided very well. Then identify another service that you think is not provided well. Compare the two and develop a list of factors that justify your decision about the quality of the services.

CHAPTER REVIEW

Project Wrap-up Discuss product and service development with other class members. Prepare a list of recommendations you would provide to companies to help them develop successful new products and services.

61

GOALS
Begin each lesson and offer an overview.

LESSON 3.1
THE PRODUCT

GOALS

DESCRIBE business and customer views of products

IDENTIFY the components of the product mix element

WHAT IS A PRODUCT?

A product or service is usually the focus of exchange activities between customers and businesses. It is the marketing mix element that most businesses consider first when planning a marketing strategy. It also is the first consideration for consumers as they determine what they plan to purchase.

A product is all the attributes, both tangible and intangible, that a business offers to customers in exchange for their money. Businesses produce products and services they think customers will want to buy in order to make a profit. Customers exchange money with businesses in order to obtain the products and services they want. Businesses and consumers have very different views of this important mix element.

ON THE $CENE

The Geofase Company is a small manufacturer of specialty athletic footwear. It makes and sells footwear for wrestlers, gymnasts, fencers, and swimmers. Other athletic shoe manufacturers are selling their products to the general public as "designer" footwear by changing designs, fabrics, and colors. Designer shoes often sell for a much higher price than traditional athletic shoes. The Geofase Company wonders if it can compete in this new market. It will cost money to develop and produce the new designs. But the higher prices and broader market could result in greater profits for the company. What information do you think Geofase needs to make the decision? What factors will influence its success with the new products?

62

ON THE SCENE
Lesson opening scenario that provides motivation.

vide information about the product. Packages are used to promote the product through the use of color, shape, images, and information. Packaging can even make the product more useful for the consumer as with children's drink boxes with attached straws and window cleaners that attach to a garden hose.

Support Services If you purchase a computer, cellular telephone, or home entertainment system today, the salesperson will probably offer you a maintenance contract. The *maintenance contract* is a support service that will pay for repair work if the product fails to operate properly. Many times the services provided with a product make the product easier to use. Customers will want to purchase support services if they are concerned they will be unable to assemble or operate a product or if they want assistance in its use.

Brand and Image A brand is a name, symbol, word, or design that identifies a product, service, or company. A brand is very important to a company because it provides a unique identification for it and its offerings. There may be a few items that you will refuse to purchase unless you can find the brand you want. With other products you aren't even aware of the brand or are satisfied with one of several available brands.

One of the major reasons for brand loyalty is the image of the brand. The brand's **image** is a unique, memorable quality of a brand. Some brands have an image of quality, others of low price, and still others as innovative. Brand image must match the important needs of the consumer to be effective.

INCREASE IN PRODUCT VALUE

When customers purchase products or services, they want to receive a good value. If the product is poorly constructed, will not work properly, or may wear out quickly, consumers may be unwilling to purchase it. Companies offer guarantees or warranties as insurance that the product will be repaired or replaced if there are problems. If a customer thinks a company will stand behind its products, they are more likely to purchase from that company.

Another way to add value is to increase the number of ways a product can be used. A classic example of expanding markets through new product uses is baking soda. Very few consumers bake their own bread today, so a baking soda manufacturer saw sales declining. The company conducted a consumer behavior study and found that consumers use baking soda for many other purposes. Some use it to freshen refrigerators, garbage disposals, and litter boxes for pets. Others use it to brush their teeth. Through promoting those and other uses, the company increased its sales dramatically.

CHECKPOINT

What are the components of the product mix element?

CHECKPOINT
Short questions within lessons to assist with reading and to assure students are grasping concepts.

WORKSHOP

Work in small groups to analyze three different products—one that costs less than $5, one that costs between $25 and $100, and one that costs more than $10,000. Prepare a chart for each product that identifies the basic product, features and options, related services, packaging features, brand and image, guarantees or warranties, and uses of the product. Compare your charts with those of other groups.

WORKSHOP
Provides activities to use in class.

65

SPECIAL FEATURES ENHANCE LEARNING

Service businesses often design a brochure to communicate the intangible features and benefits of their service to customers. Select a service business from your community. Write the copy for a brochure for the business that explains the form, timing, quality, and availability of the service.

COMMUNICATE
Provides activities to reinforce, review, and practice communication skills.

BUSINESS MATH CONNECTION
Worked example that reinforces and reviews math concepts.

Businesses calculate the *breakeven point* to determine the number of products they need to sell to cover their costs before they start making a profit. One product has fixed costs of $83,500, no matter how many units are produced. It has variable costs of $10.50 for each unit produced. The company plans to sell the product for $54.00. How many products will it have to produce and sell to break even?

SOLUTION
To find the breakeven point, divide the fixed costs by the selling price minus the variable costs. The breakeven point is 1,920 units.

Fixed costs ÷ (Selling price − Variable costs) = Breakeven point

$83,500 ÷ ($54.00 − $10.50) = 1,919.54, or 1,920 units

NET CHATS YIELD CONSUMER INFORMATION Companies have a new tool for keeping up with consumer ideas and opinions. Online chat rooms and bulletin boards on the Internet are places where groups with common interests meet to talk with each other about their experiences and opinions. Businesses can tap into those conversations to gain valuable insights that help them improve current products and develop new offerings. Hallmark Cards developed an "Idea Exchange" web site to hold online conversations with 200 selected consumers. Hallmark employees usually let the discussion develop around any topics the consumers choose. From time-to-time, the company asks chat room participants to answer questions or discuss how they use Hallmark products.

THINK CRITICALLY How can a chat room provide better information than a more traditional method such as a focus group? Why might a consumer choose to participate in a company-sponsored Internet chat room?

TECH TALK
Provides information about new technology that is being used in business.

During the period of 1986 to 1996, the number of new products introduced in supermarkets grew from 12,500 to 26,000 per year. However, only about 8 percent were truly new. The rest were improvements to existing products.

DID YOU KNOW?
Provides an interesting fact about the topic.

Dedicated web site b2000.swep.com that provides activities and links for each chapter.

b2000.swep.com

International Product Leadership

Companies must be cautious in recognizing the type of competition they face as they move into international markets. Often, businesspeople and consumers alike think businesses in their own countries are their primary competitors. However, specific countries have developed reputations as leaders in producing and marketing certain categories of products. The U.S. is recognized worldwide for its entertainment and movie industries. Japan has a reputation for producing quality automobiles. Argentina exports agricultural products. France is a leading headquarters for airplane production.

THINK CRITICALLY Why do businesspeople and consumers often fail to recognize the strong competition provided by businesses from other countries?

WORLD VIEW
Provides international business connections relevant to today's current events.

ASSESSMENT AND REVIEW

THINK CRITICALLY

1. Why is the product component usually the first to be considered by companies when they are developing a marketing mix?

2. Why is an extended product important for some products but not for others?

3. Why would a company add features to a product?

4. For what types of purchases would a warranty be very important? Why?

MAKE CONNECTIONS

5. ADVERTISING Use word-processing software to write an advertisement for a new brand of breakfast cereal bar. The product name is "All Day Energy" and the target market is 15- to 30-year-old males and females who are active, concerned about their fitness, yet have difficulty finding time to eat a complete breakfast.

6. DEBATE Some fast-food restaurants and cereal manufacturers give small toys and games to children with a food purchase. The purpose is to have children encourage their parents to buy the company's brand. Some people suggest that this results in purchases made for the wrong reasons. Organize a debate in your class using the following statement.

> Companies should not be able to use unrelated products (games and toys) as an incentive to encourage the purchase of fast food and cereal for children.

END-OF-LESSON ACTIVITIES

Think Critically Provides opportunities to apply concepts.

Make Connections Provides connections to other disciplines.

Presentation Icon indicates opportunity to use presentation software, such as PowerPoint.

Word Processing Icon indicates opportunity to use word processing software.

Spreadsheet Icon indicates opportunity to use spreadsheet software.

Internet Icon indicates opportunity to research on the web.

CHAPTER REVIEW
Contains Chapter Summary, Vocabulary Builder, Review Concepts, Apply What You Learned, Make Connections

REVIEW

CHAPTER 3

CHAPTER SUMMARY

LESSON 3.1 The Product
A. The product is the mix element that most businesses consider first when planning a marketing mix. It also is the first consideration for consumers as they determine what they plan to purchase.
B. The product or service as a marketing mix element includes anything offered to the customer by the business that will be used to satisfy needs.

LESSON 3.2 Product Planning
A. Companies can reduce the rate of product failure by improving their understanding of consumer needs and competition.
B. Businesses need a process to identify and develop new products. The process should eliminate products that are not likely to be successful. It should ensure that the products meet an important market need, can be produced at a reasonable price, and will be competitive.

LESSON 3.3 Product Life Cycles
A. Analyzing a product life cycle aids marketers in understanding its competition and developing an effective marketing mix.
B. Successful products move through predictable stages that show how profits and sales change as competition increases.

LESSON 3.4 Effective Services
A. The number of businesses providing services as their primary activity is growing faster than any other type of business.
B. Services differ from products in form, availability, quality, and timing.

VOCABULARY BUILDER

Choose the term that best fits the definition. Write the letter of the answer in the space provided. Some terms may not be used.

_____ 1. Anything offered to a market by the business to satisfy needs

_____ 2. A name, symbol, word, or design that identifies a product, service, or company

_____ 3. Assisting in the design and development of products and services that will meet the needs of prospective customers

_____ 4. The stages of sales and profit performance through which all brands of a product progress as a result of competition

_____ 5. Activities of value that do not result in the ownership of anything tangible

_____ 6. A unique, memorable quality of a brand, such as quality, low price, or innovation

_____ 7. Added to improve the basic product

_____ 8. Sample developed for expensive or risky products

a. brand
b. feature
c. image
d. product
e. product life cycle
f. product/service planning
g. prototype
h. services

REVIEW CONCEPTS

9. What are consumers most concerned about when they purchase a product?

PRINT YOUR BROWSER

b2000.swep.com

APPLY WHAT YOU LEARNED

20. Provide an example of a basic, enhanced, and extended product.

MAKE CONNECTIONS

23. ADVERTISING Select four print advertisements from magazines and newspapers that advertise a service. Choose two ads that you think are effective in helping customers understand what they will receive when they purchase the service. Choose two others that you think are ineffective. Using a computer and word processing software, write a two-page paper that explains why the first two ads were effective and why the other two were ineffective.

24. PROBLEM SOLVING Work with a team of three other students. Select a product that the team agrees is not as effective as it could be. Make a list of the product's problems. Then brainstorm to develop a new product that improves on the problems of the selected product. Create a model or an illustration of the new product to show to other team members. Present your team's model in class, explaining the improvements your team has made and the problems you were solving.

25. BUSINESS MATH A company has determined that one of its products has moved into the maturity stage of the product life cycle and is facing more intense price competition. The company is analyzing several possible price reductions to determine the effect of each on profits. Using the following table and spreadsheet software, calculate the total revenue and the profit or loss for each possible price.

26. ANALYTICAL SKILLS Large businesses often allow their customers to choose the product that best meets their needs by offering a product line. A product line may include an inexpensive choice with few features and options, a mid-priced choice with more features and options, and a full-featured, expensive choice. Surf the Internet to find an online consumer electronics store, appliance store, or furniture store. Identify a product for which the business offers at least three levels of choice in a product line. Gather information from the web site. Based on the information you gather, prepare a chart that describes the following elements

PLAN PRODUCTS AND SERVICES 60

DISTRIBUTION AND GLOBAL MARKETING 86

CHAPTER 5

PRICE SETTING 108

CHAPTER 6

PROMOTION 130

REVIEWERS

Marilyn Allen
Hazelwood, MO

Rod Belnap
Ogden, UT

Monica Caillouet
Gonzales, LA

David Corbin
Country Club Hills, IL

Sissy Long
Pensacola, FL

Vicki McKay
Pasadena, TX

Debbie Popo
Columbus, OH

Edward Pregitzer
Cincinnati, OH

Anne Jansen Wardinski
Burke, VA

CHAPTER 1

THE WORLD OF MARKETING

LESSONS

1.1 MARKETING BASICS

1.2 ECONOMICS AND MARKETING

1.3 MARKETING THEN AND NOW

1.4 MARKETING AND E-COMMERCE

PROJECT
The Importance of Marketing

PROJECT OBJECTIVES

■ Recognize the role of marketing in the U.S. economy
■ Understand how marketing meets consumer and business needs
■ Consider the variety of marketing activities performed in business
■ Identify ethical responsibilities of businesses

GETTING STARTED

Read through the Project Process below. Make a list of any materials and information you will need. Decide how you will get the needed materials or information.
■ At the top of a sheet of paper, write a one- or two-sentence definition of "marketing" in your own words.

PROJECT PROCESS

Part 1 LESSON 1.1 Make a list of all of the words you have identified that relate to marketing. Develop a description of each of the words to help you understand marketing. Compare your list and descriptions with other students.

Part 2 LESSON 1.2 In a small group, develop a list of reasons why marketing is important to businesses. Develop another list of reasons why marketing is important to consumers. Discuss what happens to businesses and consumers if marketing activities are not performed well.

Part 3 LESSON 1.3 In a small group, draw a horizontal line across the center of a large sheet of paper. Divide the line into 25-year sections starting with 1900 and ending with 2025. Using the Internet and library references, list important historical events for each 25-year period above the line. List important business and marketing events for each time period below the line. Compare your timeline with those of other groups.

Part 4 LESSON 1.4 Identify a business involved in e-commerce and find the company's web site on the Internet. After studying the web site, describe how the Internet is used as a part of the company's marketing efforts.

CHAPTER REVIEW

Project Wrap-up As a class, discuss how marketing has changed over the years and why marketing is important to both businesses and consumers.

LESSON 1.1
MARKETING BASICS

DEFINE marketing

DESCRIBE the importance of marketing to businesses, consumers, and society

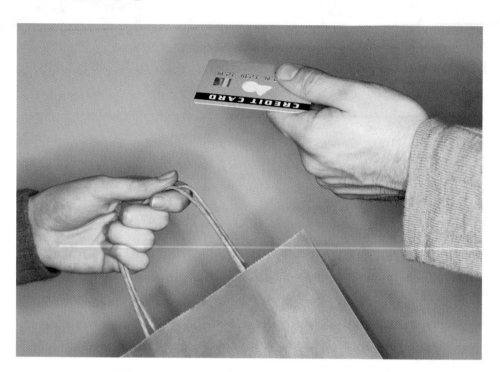

MARKETING IN YOUR LIFE

Marketing activities are a part of your life almost every day. Businesses offer a variety of products and services to meet your wants and needs. Trucks, airplanes, and ships move products all around the world so they are available for you to buy. Companies advertise those products and services to encourage you to buy. They also may offer you the opportunity to pay for purchases with a checking account or credit card. These are all examples of marketing activities. Without effective marketing, you would not have access to most of the products and services you use every day.

ON THE $CENE

As a part of a career report, Darlene must identify an area of business with careers that interest her. She has heard that marketing provides many job opportunities. However, when she thinks of marketing careers, she has images of retail clerks and automobile salespeople. She thinks the first career is low paying and the second has a poor reputation among consumers. She also thinks that both require long hours of work each week. Do you think Darlene's image of those careers is accurate? Why or why not? What other marketing careers could you suggest to Darlene?

WHAT IS MARKETING?

According to the American Marketing Association, *marketing* is the process of planning and executing the conception, pricing, promotion, and distribution of ideas, goods, and services to create exchanges that satisfy individual and organizational objectives. This definition is long and complex because of the many different types of marketing activities and the variety of businesses and other organizations that use marketing. A simpler definition of marketing describes its importance to businesses and consumers. **Marketing** develops and maintains satisfying exchange relationships between businesses and consumers.

THE ELEMENTS OF EXCHANGE

An **exchange** means that two people or organizations are involved in a transaction. Each has something the other wants, and they must agree on the value of the items they have to exchange. For the transaction to be successful, each of the participants must be satisfied with what they receive as a result of the exchange.

In marketing, a business offers a product or service for sale to consumers. Consumers have money to spend to purchase things they want or need. If the business and consumer can agree on a price, the consumer pays the company and receives the product or service from the company in exchange. The company is satisfied if it makes a profit. Consumers are satisfied if the product or service meets their needs. Many exchanges of products and services every day result in satisfaction for the business and the customer. However, some do not. One of the goals of marketing is to improve the exchange process so those involved are satisfied.

MARKETING FUNCTIONS

Marketing involves many activities. The activities are performed as products and services are planned and moved from producers to consumers. The performance of the marketing activities is the responsibility of marketers. Marketing activities can be grouped into seven functions as shown at the right. Each of these functions occurs every time a product or service is developed and sold. Marketing is a complex part of business and is very important to the success of businesses and to the satisfaction of customers.

Product/Service Management Designing, developing, maintaining, improving, and acquiring products and services so they meet customer needs.

FUNCTIONS OF MARKETING

- MARKETING-INFORMATION MANAGEMENT
- SELLING
- FINANCING
- DISTRIBUTION
- PRICING
- PRODUCT/SERVICE MANAGEMENT
- PROMOTION

Distribution Determining the best methods and procedures to be used so customers are able to locate, obtain, and use the products and services of an organization.

Selling Communicating directly with prospective customers to assess and satisfy their needs.

Marketing-Information Management Obtaining, managing, and using market information to improve business decision making and the performance of marketing activities.

Financing Budgeting for marketing activities, obtaining the necessary financing, and providing financial assistance to customers to assist them with purchasing the organization's products and services.

Pricing Establishing and communicating the value of products and services to prospective customers.

Promotion Communicating information about products and services to prospective customers through advertising and other promotional methods to encourage them to buy.

CHECKPOINT

What is a simple definition of marketing that emphasizes the needs of those involved?

_____

_____

MEETING BUSINESS AND CONSUMER NEEDS

The economic system of the United States is often referred to as a free enterprise system or market economy. That means that people are free to start a business and offer products and services for sale in competition with many other businesses. Individuals start businesses to do work they enjoy and to make a profit.

Individual consumers are free to spend their resources to purchase the products and services they want. They have many choices of products and services and the businesses they want to purchase from. Consumers generally will make the choices that provide the greatest value for the money they are spending.

MARKETING AND BUSINESSES

Marketing is an important part of business. Some people think that if a business offers a good product, marketing is not necessary. However, if customers do not know about the product, do not know where to purchase it, are unable to get to the place where it is sold, cannot afford the price of the product, or do not think the product is a good value, they will not purchase it. Marketing is required to provide a variety of activities or services so the customer will be able to purchase the product.

Marketing cannot be successful if the product is not what the customer wants or is a poor quality product. While customers may be encouraged to buy a product through advertising, selling, or a low price, they also must see the product as satisfying a need. If customers decide to buy the product and it does not work the way they were led to believe, is of poor quality, or has a defect, they will likely return the product for a refund. If customers do not return a product that was not satisfying, they are unlikely to buy the same product again.

Marketing activities help businesses provide the right products to the consumers who want and need them. Marketing makes the products available where and when customers want them and helps to make the products affordable. It provides the information consumers need to make the best choices.

MARKETING AND CONSUMERS

Think about a product you plan to buy sometime this week. You need to decide where to buy the product. If the location is convenient, it won't take much time to get to and from the store, and transportation will not be an issue. You usually select a store because you know it carries the items you need. The business has an adequate supply of the product as well as related items. The prices are clearly marked and affordable. If you need information to help with your decision, you will obtain it through advertising, information on the package, or assistance from a store employee. The store allows you to pay for your purchases with cash, check, credit, or debit card. Each of the activities described is an example of marketing. Consumers benefit from marketing because the activities make it easier to obtain the products and services they need.

Marketing benefits consumers in another way that may not be as obvious. Because marketing is continually determining what consumers like and dislike and what needs are not satisfied, improvements are made to products and services and new products are developed. As a result of marketing activities, more products are available to meet customers' needs. When large volumes of a product are produced and sold, the cost of production and marketing of each product actually declines. In many cases, marketing actually results in lower prices to the consumer. You can probably identify many examples of products where prices have declined by 50 percent or more from the time the product was first introduced.

BUSINESS MATH CONNECTION

The following table shows the price of the least expensive personal computer configured for business use over a three-year period in an office supply store. Find the price difference and the percentage difference between the Year 1 price and the Year 2 price.

Year	Processor/Hard Drive	Price
1	500 mhz/2 GB	$1800
2	733 mhz/10 GB	$1240
3	866 mhz/20 GB	$834

SOLUTION

Calculate the amount the computer price decreased from Year 1 to Year 2.

Year 1 price − Year 2 price = Price decrease
$1800 − $1240 = $560

Then calculate the percentage the Year 2 price is of the Year 1 price.

Year 2 price ÷ Year 1 price = Percentage difference
$1240 ÷ $1800 = 0.688, or 68.8%

MARKETING AND SOCIETY

Marketing helps to identify and develop new and better products and services. Many of those products and services are beneficial to society. For example, more efficient automobiles use less gasoline and cause less pollution. Products like airbags and motorcycle helmets reduce the number and severity of injuries from accidents.

Marketing improves the standard of living. The standard of living is based on the products and services available to consumers, the amount of resources consumers have to obtain the products and services, and the quality of life for consumers. Countries that have well-developed marketing systems are able to make more and better products available to consumers. Those countries also have more jobs for their citizens and higher wage scales.

Marketing has been particularly effective in improving international trade. International trade contributes many benefits to the participating countries and their consumers. Think of the number of products you buy that were produced in another country. Just as the United States is a large consumer of foreign products, many businesses in the U.S. sell products internationally.

CHECKPOINT

Identify a benefit marketing provides to businesses, to consumers, and to society.

_____

_____

THINK CRITICALLY

1. Why does marketing give you access to most of the products and services you use every day?

_____

_____

2. Which of the marketing functions do you think consumers are most familiar with? Least familiar with? Why?

_____

_____

3. Why is marketing necessary even if a company produces a good product that consumers want to purchase?

_____

_____

4. How can marketing result in a lower price for products?

_____

_____

_____

MAKE CONNECTIONS

5. **COMMUNICATION** Consumers need to know what products are available, where the product can be purchased, the price of the product, and the benefits the product will provide. Using newspapers, magazines, or other media, locate advertisements that provide each of the types of information listed for a product. Prepare your answer in a spreadsheet format.

6. **BUSINESS MATH** Using the information in the Business Math Connection on the previous page, find the percentage difference between the Year 2 price and the Year 3 price.

_____

_____

7. **SCIENCE** Using the Internet, research a product that helps reduce pollution and protect the natural environment. Determine the company that developed it and when it was first produced and marketed.

_____

_____

8. **PSYCHOLOGY** Consumers often have preferences for certain brands. Write down your favorite brand for each of the following: shoes, computer, soft drink, restaurant, blue jeans, automobile, and college. Compare your answers with other students. Discuss why you prefer the brands you listed.

_____

_____

_____

LESSON 1.2
ECONOMICS AND MARKETING

DISCUSS the role of supply and demand in marketing

IDENTIFY the four types of economic utility

ECONOMICS IS IMPORTANT

Effective marketing is based on economic principles. Marketers need to understand the relationship of supply and demand in order to develop satisfying exchanges with consumers.

THE LAW OF SUPPLY

One of the most important reasons for businesses to operate in a market economy is to make a profit. Businesses try to offer products and services that have a good chance of making a large profit. Business managers carefully consider both the costs of producing and marketing products and the prices they will be able to charge for those products. That analysis helps in determining the most profitable products or services to offer.

Economics predicts how the quantity of products and services produced will change at various prices. As the price of a product increases, producers

ON THE $CENE

Fredrico has just received his tax refund and is deciding how to use it. He has several uses in mind. He can make a down payment on a car, take a one-week vacation to an ocean resort, or save the money to help pay his college tuition next year. How would you help Fredrico decide on the use of his tax refund to make the purchase that will give him the greatest satisfaction?

will be willing to manufacture a larger quantity of the product. At lower prices, fewer products will be manufactured. This relationship between price and production decisions is known as the **law of supply**. Whenever possible, producers use their resources to provide products and services that receive the highest prices in order to increase profits.

THE LAW OF DEMAND

Economics also predicts how much consumers are willing to pay for various quantities of products or services. As the price of a product decreases, consumers will purchase a larger quantity. When the price of a product is increased, less will be demanded. This relationship between price and purchase decisions is known as the **law of demand**. Consumers want to get the maximum value for the money they spend on the products and services they purchase.

BALANCING SUPPLY AND DEMAND

In a market economy, businesses and consumers make decisions about what to produce and what to purchase independently. When the purchase decisions of many consumers of the same product are combined, they determine the quantity of the product that will be purchased and the price consumers prefer to pay. When the decisions of all the suppliers of the same product or service are combined, they determine the amount of the product that will be available for sale and the price suppliers would like to receive. If fewer products are available than consumers want to buy, the price will usually increase. If more products are available than demanded by consumers, businesses will have to

reduce the price they charge. If the quantity demanded matches the quantity supplied, both consumers and suppliers will be satisfied.

In small groups, identify products that have a very high price because of a limited supply. Then identify products with low prices because of a large supply. Discuss how the prices affect consumer perceptions of the products.

CHECKPOINT

When are supply and demand balanced in a market economy?

_____

_____

ECONOMIC UTILITY

Most people have many more products and services they would like to buy than they are able to afford. They have to make choices among the products and services they want. People attempt to purchase those that provide the greatest amount of satisfaction for the money they are able or willing to spend. You may have to choose between attending a concert and renting a movie. Your family may decide to drive to a vacation site rather than fly to save money.

An economic concept helps you predict how people will choose among available products and service. **Economic utility** is the amount of satisfaction a consumer receives from the consumption of a particular product or service. Products that provide great satisfaction have higher economic utility than those consumers find less satisfying.

Businesspeople can use the concept of economic utility to increase the likelihood that consumers will buy their products or services. There are four primary ways businesses can increase the economic utility of a product or service. Those ways are changes in form, time, place, and possession.

FORM UTILITY

The physical product provided or the service offered by a business is the primary way that consumer needs are satisfied. *Form utility* results from actual changes in the product. The construction of a product, the features provided, or the quantity in which the product is sold may make it more useable for consumers.

TIME UTILITY

A product should be available when consumers are able to obtain or use the product. *Time utility* results from making the product or service available when the customer wants it. Examples of time utility include the following.

- A bank stays open in the evening and on Saturday mornings

- A theater schedules a show in the early afternoon or late in the evening

- An auto dealership opens its service department on weekends

- A physician's office schedules physical examinations just before an athletic season

PLACE UTILITY

Just as some consumers are concerned about when a product is available, others may want to purchase or consume the product at a particular place. Making products and services available where the consumer wants them is *place utility.*

Convenience stores are successful because they are located in neighborhoods close to where consumers live. Automatic teller machines (ATMs) and drive-in windows have made banking easier because they are located in supermarkets, airports, and even on street corners. Businesses that provide mailing, photocopying, and facsimile services are becoming very popular, but they must be located conveniently to small businesses and individual consumers who need them.

POSSESSION UTILITY

Possession utility is more difficult to understand than the other three types. A product may be in the form a consumer wants and be available at the right time in the right place, yet the consumer still may not be able to purchase the product because they do not have the amount of money needed. Possession utility makes products and services more affordable. It is usually not possible for a business to decrease the price just so a product can be sold. It does not want to sell products at a loss. Yet there are other ways besides cutting the price to make a product more affordable.

Offering credit allows people to purchase things for which they do not have enough cash at the time. In a similar way, many retail businesses offer layaway services where a person can pay a small amount of the purchase price over several months and own the product after full payment is made.

Few people want to spend money to purchase a movie just so they can watch it more than once. Video stores are very successful because they rent movies rather than sell them. Automobile dealerships lease new automobiles so customers can drive new cars without having to make a huge down payment. All of these examples show how businesses can offer alternative ways for consumers to afford purchases.

COMMUNICATE

Select a familiar product. Assume you are responsible for marketing this product. Prepare a one-page sales letter about the product. In the letter, identify how each of the economic utilities is provided to meet consumer needs. Read your letter in class.

CHECKPOINT ✓

What are the four types of economic utility?

_____

_____

THINK CRITICALLY

1. Why is an understanding of supply and demand important for marketers?

_____

_____

2. Identify a product or service where it appears the quantity supplied by business and the quantity demanded by consumers is not balanced?

_____

_____

_____

3. How do consumers make decisions when they have more products and services they want to purchase than they can afford?

_____

_____

_____

4. Think of a product or service you purchase regularly. How can the business selling this product or service increase its economic utility?

_____

_____

_____

MAKE CONNECTIONS

5. **TECHNOLOGY** Changes in technology are ways that businesses are able to provide increased consumer satisfaction and sell additional products. Use the Internet to research examples of technological improvements being planned by businesses. Report your findings to the class and discuss with them whether the new technology appears to meet a consumer need.

_____

_____

_____

6. **FINANCE** Select three products that are sold in several businesses in your community. Develop a computer spreadsheet in which you list the names of businesses that sell the product. Determine the price charged by each business for the products and list the prices in your spreadsheet next to the business name. Use the spreadsheet to prepare a list of the highest prices and the lowest prices for all of the products. Calculate the total amount a consumer would have to pay for the highest priced list and the lowest priced list.

LESSON 1.3
MARKETING THEN AND NOW

THE CHANGING VIEW OF MARKETING

T he term *marketing* describes a number of different activities. Marketing is essential not only to the success of manufacturers and retailers, but also to government agencies, hospitals, law offices, schools, and churches. Successful businesses develop an approach to marketing planning so customers will be satisfied with the products and services they purchase.

Marketing was not always an important part of business. Businesses' use of marketing changed quite a bit during the twentieth century. It shifted from a focus on production, to an emphasis on promotion and selling, and finally to an increase in marketing activities provided.

ON THE $CENE

S haye walked into the Tech Boutique to purchase a new case for her cellular telephone. At first the salesperson couldn't find any cases for the model of phone Shaye owned even though she had purchased it only three months earlier at the same store. Finally the salesperson found a choice of two cases in a catalog and said he could have one available in four to seven days. However both were vinyl and Shaye wanted a leather case. Even though Shaye liked her phone, what do you think her feelings are now about Tech Boutique? If you were Shaye, what would you tell others about your experience?

CULTURAL MISTAKES

Understanding customers is particularly important in international marketing. When Coca Cola introduced its soft drink in China, the first brand name translated into Chinese as "bite the wax tadpole." The Chinese characters were immediately changed to a more appropriate meaning, "happiness in the mouth," which created a much better image.

Betty Crocker cake mixes failed when introduced in Japan. With a bit more study of consumers there, General Mills would have learned that many Japanese homes do not have ovens. The company then developed the mixes so they could be baked in rice cookers. Again the product failed because Japanese housewives thought the rice would have a bad flavor if the cooker was used to bake a cake.

THINK CRITICALLY How can companies avoid these types of marketing mistakes if they want to sell their products in other countries?

FOCUS ON PRODUCTION

In the early 1900s businesses focused on producing products that customers needed and were able to afford. Major efforts that could be considered marketing were directed at getting the products to customers. There were not many choices of transportation methods, and roads and highways were not well developed. The primary way to sell more products was to be able to deliver them to a larger number of customers.

As consumers increased their standards of living and had more money to spend, the demand for newer and better products increased. Demand was usually greater than the available supply of products. Businesspeople concentrated on production and seldom had to worry a great deal about marketing. Customers often were eager to buy new products and would seek out the manufacturer when they heard of a product they wanted.

EMPHASIS ON PROMOTION AND SELLING

Over time companies adopted more efficient production processes. They could produce a larger quantity of products. Railroad and highway systems expanded to improve transportation. Businesses had to compete with each other to get customers to buy their products. Businesses began to give more attention to basic marketing activities, such as advertising and selling, to convince customers that their products were superior to those of competitors.

INCREASE IN MARKETING ACTIVITIES

While promotion made people more aware of a company's products, it did little to actually meet customer needs. Businesses began to use a variety of marketing activities to encourage customers to buy their brand. Products were sold through more locations to make them more accessible. More efficient transportation methods such as express delivery and distribution centers moved products more quickly to consumers. To encourage customers to buy their products rather than competitors' brands, companies offered credit and discounted prices and added services and guarantees. The result was more attention to marketing but higher costs and lower profits for companies.

CHECKPOINT

Name three historical approaches to marketing businesses used in the twentieth century.

_____

_____

THE MARKETING CONCEPT

As it became more and more difficult and expensive for businesses to sell their products, some businesspeople began to realize an important fact. Businesses could no longer be successful by just producing more products, increasing the amount of advertising and selling efforts, or expanding individual marketing services.

The most successful businesses were the ones that considered customers' needs and worked to satisfy those needs as they produced and marketed their products and services. That philosophy of business is known as the marketing concept. The **marketing concept** is using the needs of customers as the primary focus during the planning, production, distribution, and promotion of a product or service.

To use the marketing concept, businesses must be able to

- Identify what will satisfy customers' needs
- Develop and market products or services that customers consider to be better than other choices
- Operate profitably

TO USE OR NOT TO USE

Businesses that do not understand the marketing concept assume they know what the customer wants. They produce the product and then use marketing activities to convince customers to purchase from them. If the products go unsold, they will increase advertising, offer discounts or sales where prices are cut, or use other gimmicks to convince customers to buy.

WORKSHOP

Working in small groups, identify several companies that appear to use the marketing concept and several that do not. Discuss what the companies that use the marketing concept do that is different from the companies that do not use the concept.

17

The extra expenses of marketing products that customers may not have a strong interest in buying can lead to reductions in profit or even losses for the business. Additionally, after purchasing the product, the customer may decide it is not what was wanted and return the product to the business. Even if they don't return the product, they will be unhappy with both the product and the company that sold it and will not likely buy from the company again.

However, you can identify many companies that understand and use the marketing concept. A bank adds extra hours to serve customers who work late or offers online banking services to Internet-savvy customers. A community center develops special programs for days that schools are not in session so students have activities to occupy their time and parents don't have to worry about what to do with their children during the work day. Colleges offer elective courses in cooperation with high schools to allow students to earn college credit prior to graduation.

In each case the services are important to the customer and can be offered profitably by the business. The result is satisfying exchange relationships and customers who return to the company time after time.

CHECKPOINT

What is meant by the marketing concept?

_____

_____

THINK CRITICALLY

1. Why did businesses not have to concentrate on marketing in the early part of the twentieth century?

_____

_____

_____

_____

2. Why might too much emphasis on promotion and selling result in dissatisfied customers?

_____

_____

_____

_____

3. How does the use of the marketing concept result in greater customer satisfaction than traditional approaches to marketing?

_____

_____

_____

_____

MAKE CONNECTIONS

4. HISTORY Use the library to gather information on a U.S. business that was successful in the early 1900s. Prepare a two-page report on the company. In the report, be sure to explain what made the company successful.

5. SOCIAL STUDIES Many products first developed in the United States have become very popular in other countries while others are not well accepted. In small groups, develop a list of products that seem to be accepted in other countries and those that are not well accepted. Use newspapers, magazines and the Internet to gather information to help you develop the lists. Review the two lists and determine factors that might affect the acceptance of products in other countries. Identify which of the factors seem to be most related to marketing. Give group presentations of your findings to the class.

6. RESEARCH Identify a product that is commonly purchased and used by students. Survey 10 students asking each to identify the reasons they buy or do not buy the product. Use a spreadsheet program to help you summarize your findings.

LESSON 1.4
MARKETING AND E-COMMERCE

DESCRIBE the growth of Internet use by consumers and businesses

IDENTIFY ways that marketing activities are completed on the Web

BUSINESS ON THE WEB

The Internet is the new home for many businesses involved in e-commerce. **E-commerce** (electronic commerce) is the exchange of goods, services, information, or other business through electronic means. It includes the use of the Internet to buy and sell products as well as to exchange business-related information, such as transmitting purchase orders electronically or advertising online. E-commerce is now a multibillion-dollar part of the economy. It won't be long before most companies and consumers will use the Internet regularly as a business tool.

ON THE $CENE

Jackson enjoyed photography. He especially liked to take pictures of the unique landscapes he saw as he traveled. He had pictures of beach and mountain scenes, farms, and city life. At the request of his friends he developed and framed many of his favorites. They purchased the pictures to hang on the walls of their homes and apartments. Jackson wondered if he could use the Internet to sell more of his framed photographs. He had a friend who could design a web page and he could convert his photos into digital images so Internet customers could view them online. Do you think Jackson could have a successful Internet business? What steps would you advise Jackson to take to start the business?

GROWTH OF THE INTERNET

Following the introduction of the World Wide Web in the late 1960s, access to the Internet has grown to an estimated 500,000,000 people around the world. Almost 50 million homes in the U.S. had access to the Internet in 2000, up from just 13 million in 1995. The U.S. leads the world in Internet use, with approximately 40 percent of all users.

Business use of the Internet is increasing rapidly as well. According to the U.S. Department of Commerce, in 1998 U.S. Internet sales to consumers totaled $8 billion. If that seems like a very large figure, compare it to the business-to-business Internet sales in the same year. Business-to-business (B2B) sales totaled $45 billion. Still, there is a great deal of room for growth in the Internet sale of products and services. The total sales to consumers represent less than 1 percent of all consumer purchases. Internet sales worldwide are expected to reach two trillion dollars by 2005 with nearly 200 million regular Internet customers.

CHOOSING TO USE THE INTERNET

The ways businesses use the Internet vary. Companies that carry out most of their business activities through the Internet are referred to as **dot.com** businesses. The name "dot.com" comes from the end of a commercial business's web address, or *.com*. Businesses that complete most of their business activities in traditional ways are referred to as **bricks and mortar** businesses. The name "bricks and mortar" suggests that the company uses stores and factories as the locations to conduct

business. Most businesses today have chosen to use the Internet as a small part of their operations. They want to take it slow and make sure they are well prepared for the new business methods.

did you KNOW?

The greatest employment area for Internet jobs is marketing. Following are some categories with the percent of jobs that are Internet-related.

Manufacturing	17%
Accounting	12%
Marketing	33%
Information Technology	28%
Management	10%

CHECKPOINT

What is the difference between a dot.com and a bricks and mortar business?

_____

_____

E-MARKETING

E-commerce is still a new method of conducting business for both companies and consumers. Most people do not currently use the Internet to purchase products. In fact, only 2 percent of Internet users say they go online with the specific intention of making a purchase. More than 80 percent say their primary reason for going online is communication. If they are interested in purchasing a specific product, consumers are more likely to use the Internet to gather information and to compare alternatives. Then many will go to a local business to make the purchase.

SUCCESS WITH E-COMMERCE

The primary reasons consumers report that they do not shop online are security concerns, difficulty in making purchases using the Internet, and a belief that they will receive poor customer service if they have problems with the order or the product. Businesses need to reassure customers that their shopping experience will be positive and trouble-free.

Online shoppers often are very loyal to specific businesses and brands. They usually prefer to shop at the same businesses and buy the same brands they have traditionally purchased. However, they will switch to other businesses and brands if the online shopping experience is not satisfactory.

Reasons Customers Use an Internet Business	Reasons Customers Do Not Use an Internet Business
An understandable, easy-to-use web site	Slow response time in providing information or processing orders
Familiar businesses and brand names	A web site that is slow or often does not work
Useful and accurate information	Out-of-date or limited information
Assurance of security	Poor customer service

EFFECTIVE INTERNET MARKETING

When information about a company's products and services can be viewed by people in many locations, it is especially important for the business to identify its customers and understand their needs and wants. The business must be able to offer the products and services that customers want, but also must be able to distribute them effectively, make purchases affordable and easy for the customers to order and make payments, and provide information in the form of descriptions and pictures to answer important customer questions. Several marketing functions are particularly important in e-commerce.

Marketing-Information Management The Internet has improved the ability of businesses to gather information on current and prospective customers. Information requests, purchases, and product registrations allow companies to collect important information about the customer, including address, telephone number, and even an e-mail address. Information can be obtained on where customers purchase their products, reasons for purchasing the product, and whether the customer owns or plans to purchase related products. The information can improve the company's ability to provide improved products for their customers in the future.

Information about competitors is easier to obtain using the Internet. Businesses put a great deal of information about their products and operations on the Web. It is relatively easy to learn about competitors' products, prices, credit terms, distribution policies, and the types of customer services offered.

Distribution Companies that have integrated product purchasing into their web sites make it possible for customers to order products online. Online shopping carts have been designed to make it easy to complete an order, make immediate payment using a credit card, and submit the order securely to the company.

The Internet does not necessarily improve the physical handling and distribution of products. Many products need to be shipped to the customer by truck, airplane, railroad, or ship. However, many services and some products actually can move from producer to consumer online. In some cases, the use of the Internet makes it easier and much less expensive to distribute products. Customers can download software from a company's web site rather than purchasing a CD or diskettes. Taxpayers can go online to access forms and instructions from government web sites. Newspapers and magazines have created online editions of their publications. Airlines and travel agencies have developed e-tickets so paper tickets are no longer needed for travel. Publishers have created electronic books (e-books) that can be downloaded and read on specially designed computer viewers.

Future technologies will likely make it possible for even more products and services to be distributed using computers and the Internet. As customers get more familiar and comfortable with the Internet, they will purchase more and more products online.

Promotion The purpose of promotion as a marketing activity is to communicate information in order to encourage customers to purchase the business's products and services. Because consumers use the Internet for communications, promotion is an effective use of the Internet by businesses.

Both bricks and mortar and dot.com businesses can benefit from using the Internet for promotion. Online advertising by bricks and mortar businesses allows prospective customers to easily gather information and make purchase decisions before visiting the store. Dot.com businesses can use advertising to encourage customers to make online purchases rather than going to a traditional business.

The Internet also offers other ways to reach prospective customers and promote products. Four primary methods include online advertisements, web site sponsorship, priority placement in web browsers and comparison shopping services, and providing consumer information web sites.

ONLINE OR IN-STORE Many experienced retailers have developed web sites to serve Internet shoppers. They also offer kiosks to extend the advantages of computer shopping to their in-store consumers. Kiosks are computer terminals set up in stores that allow customers to browse for products online. Kiosks often are very visible and attractively designed with computers and keyboards. They may be built into displays or placed in a comfortable seating area. Some kiosks have touch screens with easy-to-follow on-screen instructions. In-store kiosks achieve some amazing results. As a part of a major store redesign program, Kmart installed 3,500 kiosks nationwide connected to their BlueLight.com web site. Within five months, they found that 20 percent of the Internet business was coming from inside Kmart stores. Barnes and Noble has seen book sales jump dramatically as a result of giving customers in-store access to computer terminals.

THINK CRITICALLY What are some advantages of using kiosks for traditional bricks and mortar retailers?

Just as with other types of advertising, companies compete on the Web for the attention of Internet users. They try to place their advertisements on pages that prospective customers are most likely to visit. They also use creative advertising designs. Varied sizes, colors, and placements of advertisements encourage Internet users to stop and read the company's information.

An effective way to build recognition of a company's name and products with customers who are likely to purchase those products is to sponsor a related informational web site. The sponsor's name is included on the web site so visitors see the name each time they access the site.

Businesses have developed many other ways to communicate with Internet users to promote their products and services. The business can use e-mail to send special offers, new product information, or other communications to customers. You may have seen online coupons that are similar to the coupons you receive in the mail or that are printed in newspapers and magazines. They are used either by printing and mailing the coupon with an order or by entering a special code on the order form when purchasing online.

Internet promotions are used to encourage consumers to request free samples, send for detailed product information, or visit a local store where the company's products are sold. Advanced technology allows businesses to provide three-dimensional views of their products online for detailed examination by the customer.

Name three marketing functions that are important in e-commerce.

_____

_____

THINK CRITICALLY

1. Why does e-commerce currently account for such a small percentage of all consumer purchases?

_____

_____

_____

2. Why have a few dot.com businesses been successful while many have not?

_____

_____

_____

3. Name several reasons customers choose to make purchases online.

_____

_____

_____

4. What are the types of ways that the Internet is used for communication by consumers? By businesses?

_____

_____

_____

_____

MAKE CONNECTIONS

5. TECHNOLOGY Security is an important issue for consumers before they will make purchases using the Internet. Visit several business sites on the Internet. Identify the ways that the business provides security for customer orders and how it tries to assure customers about that security. Discuss your findings with other class members.

6. GOVERNMENT For many years, the federal government did not allow state and local governments to collect sales tax on Internet purchases made by customers from other states. This was done to encourage the growth of Internet sales. Bricks and mortar businesses considered that policy to be unfair, because they must collect the sales tax. Form teams and debate whether Internet sales should be subject to the same taxes as sales made by other businesses.

7. COMMUNICATION Advertisements on the Internet appear in various sizes and shapes with color, graphics, and even movement. Advertisements must attract the attention of Internet users and provide information that will encourage the consumer to purchase the company's product or service. Use the Internet to identify one advertisement you think is effective and one that you think is ineffective. Make copies of the advertisements using a computer graphics or presentation program. Present the advertisements to other students and explain why you think each is effective or ineffective.

REVIEW

CHAPTER SUMMARY

LESSON 1.1 Marketing Basics

A. Marketing is successful when customer needs are satisfied and when a business makes a profit.

B. In a market economy, consumers have many choices of products and services and the businesses to purchase from.

LESSON 1.2 Economics and Marketing

A. Effective marketing is based on economic principles. Marketers need to understand the relationship of supply and demand.

B. Businesspeople can use the concept of economic utility to increase the likelihood that consumers will buy their products or services.

LESSON 1.3 Marketing Then and Now

A. Marketing is more complex and important to businesses than in the past.

B. The most successful businesses are those that work to satisfy customers' needs as they produce and market their products and services.

LESSON 1.4 Marketing and E-Commerce

A. E-commerce is now a multibillion-dollar part of our economy. While currently less than one percent of all business sales are completed using the Internet, that figure is growing rapidly.

B. In order to be successful on the Internet, businesses need to reassure customers that the shopping experience will be positive and trouble-free.

VOCABULARY BUILDER

Choose the term that best fits the definition. Write the letter of the answer in the space provided. Some terms may not be used.

_h_ **1.** Developing and maintaining satisfying exchange relationships between businesses and consumers

_e_ **2.** When two people or organizations are involved in a transaction

_g_ **3.** The relationship between price and production decisions

_f_ **4.** The relationship between price and purchase decisions

_i_ **5.** The amount of satisfaction a consumer receives from the consumption of a particular product or service

_c_ **6.** The exchange of goods, services, information, or other business through electronic means

_b_ **7.** A company that does almost all of its business activities through the Internet

_a_ **8.** Businesses that complete most of their business activities in traditional ways rather than on the Web

a. bricks and mortar

b. dot.com

c. e-commerce

d. economic utility

e. exchange

f. law of demand

g. law of supply

h. marketing

i. marketing concept

REVIEW CONCEPTS

9. Why do businesses and consumers participate in exchanges?

because money and products are exchanged.

POINT YOUR BROWSER

b2000.swep.com

10. What are the seven functions of marketing?

distribution, selling, marketing info mgmt, financing, pricing, promotion, product/service management.

11. Why is it important to have a balance of supply and demand for a product?

because if it is balanced, both the businesses and consumers will be satisfied.

12. What are the four types of economic utility?

form, place, time, possesion.

13. Why types of marketing activities were used by businesses in the early part of the twentieth century?

early businesses focused on producing products that customers needed and could afford.

14. What three activities must be performed by businesses if they want to use the marketing concept successfully?

* identify what will satisfy customers' needs
* develop + market products.
* operate profitabily

15. What are the primary reasons that consumers do not use the Internet to make purchases?

They may not have been secure

16. What types of products can be distributed using the Internet?

Anything that can't be moved my mail

APPLY WHAT YOU LEARNED

17. Why is the satisfaction of customers and businesses an important part of marketing?

_____

_____

_____

_____

18. What will be the result if a business does not understand the laws of supply and demand when determining how many products to produce and what prices to charge?

_____

_____

_____

_____

19. Why do you think that some businesses do not understand and use the marketing concept?

_____

_____

_____

_____

20. What types of businesses do you think will be most successful in using the Internet? What types will be least successful?

_____

_____

_____

_____

MAKE CONNECTIONS

21. BUSINESS MATH In 2000, a University of Texas study reported that 3,088,000 people were employed in Internet-related jobs. Calculate the total number of people employed in Internet jobs for each category below. Using spreadsheet software, prepare a table and pie chart of your findings.

Job Category	Percent Internet	Number of Jobs
Manufacturing	17%	_____
Accounting	12%	_____
Marketing	33%	_____
Information Technology	28%	_____
Management	10%	_____

22. PROBLEM SOLVING Retail businesses often sell the same or very similar products, so customers often shop to find the lowest price and then buy the product from that business. It appears that the only way competitors can attract customers back to their stores is to lower the prices they charge. What is likely to happen to the businesses and their products if the only way they can compete is to lower the prices of products? Are there ways that retail stores can attract customers other than lowering prices? Under what circumstances do you think customers will pay more than they would have to pay for the same product in another store? Write a one- or two-page report that includes the answers to these questions.

23. ETHICS A toy manufacturer produced a large number of small children's toys that were to be given away by a fast-food chain with the purchase of any menu item. However, the toy was found to be unsafe for children under five years of age, and the federal government ordered the company not to distribute the product. It is possible that the toys could be distributed in other countries that do not have the same safety laws as the U.S. By selling the toys in another country at a very low price, the producer could recover some of the $3 million dollars already spent to manufacture the toys. Identify the ethical dilemma faced by the company's manager. Present your recommendations for solving this dilemma in class.

_____

_____

_____

_____

_____

24. CAREERS Careers in marketing require different levels of education and experience and have quite different duties. Find several marketing careers that match your interests and abilities. Make a list of the seven marketing functions identified in Lesson 1.1. Using career information you find in your school's library, career center, or the Internet, identify one job that relates to each of the functions. Identify the marketing function, the job title, the level of education required, and the expected salary range for each job.

_____

_____

_____

_____

_____

CHAPTER 2

MEET CUSTOMER NEEDS

CAREERS IN MARKETING

MARRIOTT INTERNATIONAL

Marriott International, Inc., is the world's leading hospitality company. The company, best known for its Marriott Hotels, also owns Ritz Carlton, Ramada International, and several other hotel brands. Marriott also offers vacation opportunities and meeting space.

Marriott builds and manages communities for senior citizens. It also operates a nationwide food distribution system and provides food services in colleges, corporations, and airlines.

The Manager of International Public Relations works with Marriott hotels worldwide as well as sales offices and sales agents. The manager oversees market-based public relations programs and coordinates special events for specific Marriott brands worldwide.

For this position, you need a B.A. in public relations or journalism, four or more years experience in publicity program development, and two years as a PR account manager. Exceptional writing ability and sensitivity to cultural differences are a must. Organization, time management skills, and event planning experience also are important.

THINK CRITICALLY

1. What types of special event sponsorship would benefit Marriott?
2. How would you show sensitivity to cultural differences in a resume?

PROJECT
Understand Customer Needs

PROJECT OBJECTIVES

- Understand the parts of a marketing strategy
- Recognize the need for marketing information and research
- Describe consumer decision making
- Identify examples of business-to-business marketing

GETTING STARTED

Read through the Project Process below. Make a list of materials and information you will need. Decide how you will get the needed materials or information.

- Form a small group with other students to complete the project.
- As a team, select a product for which you will make marketing decisions.

PROJECT PROCESS

Part 1 LESSON 2.1 For the product you select, describe two possible target markets that have needs for the product.

Part 2 LESSON 2.2 Make a list of the customer information you would need to effectively market your product. For each type of information, briefly describe how you would attempt to gather that information.

Part 3 LESSON 2.3 Using one target market, identify a need the consumers have that can be satisfied with the product, how the target market would normally gather information about possible choices, and where they might shop for the product.

Part 4 LESSON 2.4 Identify the types of businesses that would be involved in producing and marketing the product from the time it is developed until it is sold to the final consumer.

CHAPTER REVIEW

Project Wrap-up Develop a detailed description of the target market you would choose for your product. Also describe each of the four elements of the marketing mix you believe would be successful in meeting the needs of the consumers while making a profit for the company. Discuss your decisions with other teams.

LESSON 2.1
MARKETING STRATEGY

IDENTIFY the parts of a marketing strategy

DESCRIBE each of the elements of a marketing mix

IMPLEMENT THE MARKETING CONCEPT

The marketing concept has changed the way businesses operate. More than just a new way to complete marketing activities, it requires companies to change their approach to business planning. The marketing concept uses the needs of customers as the primary focus during the planning, production, distribution, and promotion of a product or service. That may seem simple, but the experience of many businesses shows how difficult it actually is.

Businesses fail every day because they don't understand and use the marketing concept. Any business that does not study customer needs or that is unwilling to use that information when planning and marketing products and services is taking a big risk.

ON THE $CENE

Xin Junming, an exchange student in the U.S. from China, was preparing to celebrate the Chinese New Year. The tenth night of the 15-day celebration is a time to invite friends for dinner. Junming wanted to introduce a few of his classmates to his cultural traditions. He looked in several stores for appropriate decorations representing the Year of the Horse. Even though there was a sizeable Chinese population in the town, he had no success. Whenever he would ask a clerk, he would be shown decorations used for the typical Western New Year's celebrations. Why do many businesses fail to provide products for customers with unique needs like Xin Junming?

The experiences of those businesses illustrate the difficulty of implementing the marketing concept. Most businesses spend a great deal of time and resources developing a good product or service. Yet they find that many customers do not value their product so the product fails. There are several reasons companies are frequently unsuccessful.

1. They focus too much on the product or service they are developing.

2. They believe that they know what customers will buy and so fail to study the market.

3. They do not use all of their marketing tools effectively.

DEVELOP A MARKETING STRATEGY

Most businesses use carefully prepared plans to guide their operations. A company's plan that identifies how it will use marketing to achieve its goals is called a **marketing strategy**. The marketing strategy a business uses provides the clearest indication of whether that business understands the marketing concept.

Without the marketing concept, a business will develop a product or service and then decide how to market the product. There will be little consideration of who the customers are or what their needs are until the product is ready to be sold. The business expects that most people are potential customers of the product and that with adequate marketing those customers can be convinced to buy the product.

Using the marketing concept, a very different strategy will be followed. The company believes it will be most successful if it can respond to needs of customers. It also recognizes that those needs may be different among various groups of customers. The company will begin its planning by identifying potential customers and studying the needs of those customers.

The results of that study will be used to plan the products and services the company will offer. The company will attempt to develop products and services that respond to customers' needs rather than what the company thinks should be offered. Marketing and product planning will occur at the same time, involving many people in all parts of the company. Marketing will be directed at meeting the identified needs of the customers rather than developing ways to convince people to buy something they may not need.

A TWO-STEP PROCESS

Companies that follow the marketing concept operate differently from those that do not. Businesses using the marketing concept use a two-step process to develop their marketing strategy.

Identify a Target Market The first step is to identify the market. A **market** refers to a broad group of prospective customers that a company wants to serve. For example, a market for a clothing manufacturer is people who purchase apparel for outdoor work or recreation.

A company usually will not be able to meet the needs of everyone in a market and particularly not with the same product. Therefore, a company will select one or more target markets. A **target market** is a smaller group or segment of a market in which customers have similar characteristics and needs. A target market for the clothing manufacturer is workers in hazardous

BUSINESS MATH CONNECTION

A company has a choice of serving a large market of 850,000 prospective customers or a specific target market that includes 175,000 people. If it offers the product to the larger market, it estimates 23% of the market will purchase its product and each customer will spend an average of $38. If it offers a more specific product to the target market, it estimates 83% of the market will purchase its product and each customer will spend an average of $56. Calculate the amount of revenue the company can expect to receive from each market. Which strategy may provide a greater profit?

SOLUTION

To find the number of customers, multiply the total market by the percent estimated to purchase the product.

Number of customers × Average sale = Revenue
Large market: (850,000 × 0.23) × $38 = $7,429,000
Target market: (175,000 × 0.83) × $56 = $8,134,000

The target market strategy may provide a greater profit.

occupations who need protective clothing. Another target market could be people who enjoy hiking and camping and want lightweight apparel appropriate for changes in temperature and weather. Companies that follow the marketing concept conduct extensive marketing research to gather and analyze consumer information. They use this information to classify customers according to similar characteristics, needs, and purchasing behavior.

Develop a Marketing Mix The second step in a marketing strategy is to develop a marketing mix that will meet the needs of the target market and that the business can provide profitably. A **marketing mix** is the blending of four marketing elements—product, distribution, price, and promotion.

Companies that follow the marketing concept use the needs of the target market to develop a marketing mix that will satisfy those customers. A company can decide to serve more than one target market. However, because every target market has unique needs, each will require a different marketing mix. The workers in hazardous occupations will need very different types of clothing than the people involved in outdoor recreation. Not only will the clothing products differ for each group but so will the places and methods used to sell the clothing to each group of customers. Prices charged and the promotional methods and messages used will differ as well.

CHECKPOINT

What are two steps in developing a marketing strategy?

PLAN A MARKETING MIX

A business uses the marketing concept because it believes that the best decisions can be made when the needs of consumers become an important focus of the planning. By combining the planning of product, distribution, pricing, and promotion, a company has the best opportunity to develop a satisfying, competitive, and profitable mix. Businesspeople need to understand each of the mix elements and all of the choices available in order to develop a good marketing mix.

Product When the term *product* is used, you may think of the company's basic offering that is similar to what is sold by many other competitors, such as a movie, a boat, a meal at a restaurant, or an item of clothing. However, there is much more to the product. Each competitor must make decisions that will make its brand different from and better than those offered by competitors.

Parts of the product decision that can improve customer satisfaction are special features such as a unique design, construction, size, color, or operation. Accessories can be added to make the product easier to operate, more efficient, and so on.

Products can be improved with the availability of service to customers. Services can be provided before or after the sale. They can relate to the purchase, delivery, installation, use, or maintenance of the product. Guarantees and warranties should be considered a part of the product because they make customers more confident in the purchase.

Packaging is an important part of the product. A package often is needed to protect the product. It also can make the product easier to use and provide important information for the customer.

Distribution Distribution has an important impact on satisfaction. It makes the product available where and when the customer wants it. You may have purchased a product that was damaged during shipment, poorly packaged, or assembled incorrectly. That certainly caused some inconvenience and may have caused you to return the product and purchase it from another company.

Usually distribution involves several companies as products move from producer to consumer. Manufacturers must rely on wholesalers and retailers to sell their products. Retailers must locate and obtain the products their customers want. Try to trace the channel of distribution for products you purchase. Sometimes it is almost impossible to identify the companies involved in some part of the distribution process or even the company that manufactured the product. Even though many of the businesses are not obvious to the consumer, each business performs activities that are important to the success of the marketing process. Activities such as order processing, product handling, transportation, and inventory control must be completed well if customers are to be satisfied with the products they purchase.

did you KNOW?

Nearly 20,000 new products are introduced in supermarkets each year. The three categories in which the most products are introduced are health and beauty products, condiments, and candy and snacks. On average only 1 in 4 of these new products are successful.

Pricing Price is probably the most difficult marketing decision to understand and plan. Theoretically, price is determined from the interaction of supply and demand. That relationship is important in setting the best price, but it is almost impossible to set the price of a specific product in a specific business using supply and demand. Businesses must develop specific procedures to set prices that are competitive and allow the business to make a profit. Many businesses set their prices so they will be the same or slightly lower than their major competitors. That may be necessary in some situations but also can create problems.

Calculating the price to charge involves several elements. Production, marketing, and operating costs make up a great percentage of the price of most products, so the net profit available is very small. If all of the components of a price are not considered, or if prices are not calculated carefully, businesses may find that there is no profit available after expenses have been tallied.

At times, businesses may decide to offer discounts to some or all of their customers. Sales and coupons are other ways that prices can be changed. Finally, credit commonly is offered to enable customers to purchase a product even if they don't have cash available at the time they make the purchase.

In pricing products and services, marketers must try to balance the costs of the product with the customer's feelings about the value of the product. The goal is a fair price and a reasonable profit.

Promotion When planning promotion, businesspeople select from a variety of methods. The most common are advertising, personal selling, sales promotion, visual display, and publicity. The selection will be based primarily on the company's communication objectives and the audience it wants to reach. Each method varies in terms of the cost per person, number of people reached, types of messages carried, and other factors. Careful planning needs to be done to reach the specific audience with a straightforward message in a way that helps the consumer make appropriate decisions.

Promotion cannot do much to help a company that has a poor product, excessively high prices, or ineffective distribution. Companies that have otherwise made good decisions need to have an effective promotional plan to help consumers decide from among the many choices available to them.

WORKSHOP

Visit a store and select a product for analysis. Based on your study, (1) identify the target you believe the product is directed to, and (2) describe the marketing mix being used for the product. Draw pictures on a poster board or a large sheet of paper illustrating your decisions and present them in class.

CHECKPOINT

Name the four elements of the marketing mix.

_____

_____

_____

THINK CRITICALLY

1. Why are businesses more likely to fail if they do not use the marketing concept?

You might have a bunch of junk nobody wants.

2. Why is it important to identify a target market before developing a marketing mix?

You want to identify the needs of the customer

3. Provide examples of several products for which packaging is an important part of the product mix element.

Toys

4. In what ways can promotion be misused by a company when marketing a product?

Targeting the wrong group

MAKE CONNECTIONS

5. **ART** You are responsible for designing a package for a new brand of spaghetti. The package needs to offer adequate product protection, be attractive, and communicate needed nutritional information, directions for use, and other important information. Use heavy stock paper and art supplies to create a package design. Present your package in class.

6. **BUSINESS MATH** The following chart shows the markups on the price of a product taken by businesses that are a part of a channel of distribution. Each markup is calculated on the price that a business paid for the product. Use a spreadsheet to determine the price customers will pay for each product.

Product	Production Cost	Manufacturers' Markup	Wholesalers' Markup	Retailers' Markup	Customers' Price
A	$0.58	63%	22%	46%	
B	$3.26	27%	18%	30%	
C	$25.10	12%	6%	21%	
D	$78.00	22%	11%	50%	
E	$3,220.00	6%	9%	18%	

LESSON 2.2
MARKETING RESEARCH

GOALS

IDENTIFY information you need to make marketing decisions

DESCRIBE marketing research procedures

MARKETING INFORMATION

Would you select a college or choose a career without gathering information? If you did, you might end up with a decision you would regret. As you consider a college or a job, what information will help you make the best choice? What are your interests? What preparation and resources will you need? Do you want or need to live close to your current home, or would you prefer to move to a new location? Do you have to consider the needs and opinions of other people, or will it be entirely your own decision? If you don't like your original choice, how difficult will it be to make a change after a few months or a few years?

Businesses that understand the marketing concept also recognize the value of information. By carefully determining the information they need to plan

ON THE $CENE

Movies Plus is a new 32-screen theater complex opening in a regional mall. The theater owners want the best possible experience for consumers. They also want the theater to be profitable. A survey of prospective customers found that moviegoers do not like a long walk to the lobby area to purchase snacks and they believe that theaters often are unsanitary due to the snack wrappers, food packages, and drink cups dropped on the floor. How can the theater respond to the customer concerns in the survey?

and market products, they will have a much greater chance of success than if they go forward without any information. Remember that in the past businesses relied on their experience rather than information to decide what products to produce and how to market them. That often led to dissatisfied customers, products that remained unsold, and financial loss. Today, businesses recognize the importance of careful planning, including gathering various types of information to help them make correct decisions.

TYPES OF INFORMATION

Businesses collect information for many reasons, which can all be summarized into two statements. Effective marketing information *improves the decisions of businesses* and *reduces the risk of decision making.*

If a business can make better decisions that increase the likelihood of making a profit, the time and money spent gathering information will be a good investment. More information is available to a business than it can reasonably obtain and analyze. Therefore, managers need to consider the types of information they need to make the best possible decisions. The information needed to make marketing decisions can be divided into three categories, including information about customers, the business, and the business environment.

Oustomer Information The marketing strategy of a business identifies a target market and develops a marketing mix to meet the needs of that market. Information on prospective customers is used to select the best target markets. To select a target market, a business needs to know the following.

1. What are the *characteristics* of prospective customers? Characteristics describe the customers so the business can locate them and recognize how they are different from other consumers who are not in the target market. Important characteristics of customers include age, gender, race or ethnicity, education level, geographic location, income, and occupation.

2. What are customers' *needs and wants?* Needs and wants motivate behavior. One way people attempt to satisfy their needs and wants is to purchase products and services. If people are hungry and thirsty, they look for food and beverages. If people want to socialize, they look for entertainment alternatives. Differences in needs and wants and their importance to customers help to determine the type of marketing mix a business will use to satisfy the needs and wants.

3. What *shopping behavior* do customers use to satisfy their needs? Customers use information and experience to choose the products and services they will buy. They have preferences of stores and brands. They look to different sources for information to help them decide what to buy. Understanding customer attitudes and the way they shop and select products and services will help the business make better marketing decisions.

Business Information To be able to develop an effective marketing mix, the business must understand its strengths and weaknesses, the resources it has available for product development and marketing, and what support it needs from other businesses. The type of information the business needs to collect includes the following.

■ *Performance information* How effective has the company been in the past with target markets and marketing mixes? What have been the levels of customer satisfaction, sales, and profits?

■ *Resources* What resources are available to design and develop new products? How can the company distribute products and services? Can the company offer credit and financing to customers? Does the company have expertise in communications and promotion?

■ *Support needed* Where can the company obtain needed products, services, and materials? What businesses will cooperate with the business in providing a marketing mix that meets customer needs including distribution, credit and finance, and promotion activities?

The Business Environment Businesses operate in a competitive environment. Other businesses attempt to sell similar products and services to the same customers. Understanding competitors' strengths and weaknesses will help the business develop a marketing mix that meets customer needs better than the competition. Other information about the business environment needed to make effective marketing decisions includes the following.

■ Strength of the economy

■ Laws or regulations that will affect the sale of products

■ Technology that can be used in the marketing mix

SOURCES OF INFORMATION

After a company determines the information it needs to plan a marketing strategy, the next step is to determine where the information can be obtained. Marketing information can come from internal sources, external sources, and marketing research. Marketing research will be discussed in the next section of this lesson.

Internal Information A great deal of information flows through a business. Much of it is valuable for marketing decision making. Examples of important internal information for marketing planning are listed below.

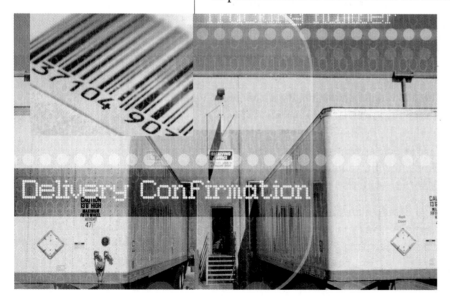

■ *Customer records and sales information* Many companies keep a complete record of all transactions they have with a customer. They record what is purchased, dates, and quantities purchased.

■ *Production and operations reports* Production and operations activities are important to marketing. Internal records provide information about sales, costs, inventory levels, and production and delivery schedules to help plan marketing mixes.

■ *Performance information* The success of a business is judged by its performance. The types of performance measures important to most businesses are sales, costs, quality, and customer satisfaction. Performance is typically measured in one of three ways. The current sales or costs can be compared to those of a previous month or year to determine if performance is improving. Performance can be compared with that of similar businesses. Or actual performance can be compared with expected performance.

External Information Marketing regularly involves other people and businesses. A business must understand and know how to work effectively with those outside the organization. External information provides an understanding of factors outside of the organization. Several valuable sources of external information include the following.

- *Government reports* An important activity of federal, state, and local governments is to supply information that can be used by businesses and consumers. There are a number of agencies that regularly collect information that can help businesses improve their marketing decisions. There are literally thousands of other databases, reports, and information sources available from government offices. Much federal government data can now be accessed through links at its comprehensive information web site at www.FedStats.gov.

- *Trade and professional associations* Trade and professional associations are organized to serve people and businesses with common interests. Most associations provide information specific to the needs of their members. That information may be disseminated through journals, newsletters, or more detailed research reports. Some associations have research services, libraries, or data services that can be used by members.

- *Business publications* Magazines and journals provide useful information for businesspeople. Those publications include general business newspapers and magazines such as *The Wall Street Journal, Forbes,* and *Business Week,* as well as more specialized publications. Business publications are useful sources of current information on the economy, legislation, new technology, or business ideas. Often the publications devote specific issues or sections to analysis of business performance.

- *Commercial data and information services* A number of businesses collect, analyze, and sell data. Dun & Bradstreet and Equifax provide credit information on consumers and businesses. A.C. Nielsen Co. and Hoover's Inc. conduct research and sell information on a number of business issues.

CHECKPOINT

What are the three categories of information businesses need to make effective marketing decisions?

_____

_____

WORKSHOP

A large discount warehouse wants to know if the location of a new product in the store affects the amount of sales in the first week. Work with a small group to design a marketing research study on this issue. Follow the scientific problem-solving procedure and use one of the three methods of marketing research to plan the study.

MARKETING RESEARCH

A business should regularly gather and analyze information in order to plan marketing strategies and make improvements in marketing procedures. Having regular access to important information will help marketers make decisions accurately and effectively.

However, sometimes a business needs information that is not currently available. The company may be considering entering a new market or a new competitor enters an existing market. In these situations, the company may not have needed information from current internal and external sources. The company will need to use marketing research to gather the information. **Marketing research** is a procedure designed to identify solutions to a specific marketing problem through the use of scientific problem-solving.

The scientific method is used to ensure that a careful and objective procedure is followed in order to develop the best possible solution. The scientific problem-solving steps used in marketing research are listed below.

1. Define the problem

2. Analyze the situation

3. Develop a data-collection procedure

4. Examine and organize information

5. Propose a solution

ORGANIZE A STUDY

Marketing research is used when a business needs to solve a specific problem. Therefore, the first step in the process is to be certain that *the problem is clearly and carefully defined.* That is not always an easy step. The problem must be stated clearly so it is understandable. The problem should be specific enough that researchers know what to study, whom to involve in the study, and the types of solutions that might be appropriate.

Analyzing the situation allows the researcher to identify what is already known about the problem, the information currently available, and the possible solutions that have already been attempted. It is possible that a careful situation analysis may result in the identification of a solution. If the decision maker is confident in the proposed solution, the marketing research process will come to an end.

After thoroughly reviewing the situation and the available information, the researcher *develops a data-collection procedure.* The researcher decides what additional information is needed and how it should be collected. The researcher needs to know where to obtain information and the best and most efficient ways to obtain the information.

After the study is complete, the researchers *examine and organize the information collected.* That information may be in the form of answers to surveys, observations that have been recorded, or data collected from an experiment. The information needs to be meaningful and easy to understand in order to solve the identified problem.

The purpose of marketing research is to identify the best strategy for the company to follow in implementing and improving marketing activities. After the research results have been organized, they need to be studied to determine if the findings support the proposed solution or suggest a different solution. Market researchers usually do not make decisions about solutions. They prepare a report of the research results which *proposes a solution* to managers. It is important that results are accurately communicated in the report. The marketing managers use the results to help them with decision making.

METHODS OF MARKETING RESEARCH

Marketing researchers gather information in several ways. The most common methods are surveys, observations, and experiments.

Surveys A survey is a planned set of questions to which individuals or groups of people respond. The survey can be completed in writing or orally. People can be surveyed in person, through the mail, by telephone, by e-mail or online messaging, or even interactive television. With some methods, consumers are presented questions on a computer or television screen. They may key responses on the computer keyboard, push buttons on a special keypad provided by the researcher, or enter information on a touch-tone telephone.

Observations An observation collects information by recording peoples' actions without interacting or communicating with the participant. The purpose of observation research is to watch the actions of the participant rather than ask them about their ideas and opinions. This usually results in greater accuracy and objectivity. However, using observations to gather data normally requires greater time and expense than surveys. The observation method often is used when collecting information about the product preferences of children.

Experiments The most precise and objective information is obtained through experimentation. Experiments are tightly controlled situations in which all important factors are the same except the one being studied. Scientific research is done by planning and implementing experiments and then recording and analyzing the data obtained to determine the result, if any, of the change.

Marketing experiments can be used to choose among target markets or to study marketing mix alternatives. For example, experiments are used to test two different locations for a retail store in a city. They also may be used to determine whether an advertisement placed on the Internet is more effective in maintaining customers' memory of a product than the traditional newspaper advertisement.

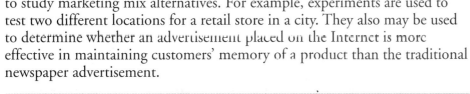

What are three methods marketing researchers use to collect information?

_____

_____

THINK CRITICALLY

1. Why is information especially important to companies that follow the marketing concept?

   What consumers want before you produce anything.

2. What is meant by the statement, "marketing information reduces the risk of decision making?"

   Make a better decision

3. How can information on whether the economy is strong or weak affect decisions about a company's marketing strategy?

   If economy is strong, then you have a bigger market, and the opposite

4. Why should companies be cautious about using information obtained from a consumer survey in making marketing decisions?

   Things change quickly, only certain people get surveyed.

MAKE CONNECTIONS

5. **TECHNOLOGY** Changes in technology not only allow companies to improve their products but also can be used to improve marketing functions. Use business magazines, your own observations of business operations, and the Internet to identify changes in technology that have improved each of the following marketing functions, including distribution, pricing, financing, selling, and promotion.

6. **GOVERNMENT** Businesses gather a lot of information about consumers as part of their marketing research activities. Many companies sell the information they collect to other companies. There is continuing discussion about whether federal and state governments should regulate how companies can use information they collect or whether businesses should regulate themselves. Use the Internet to gather information on this issue. Develop a one-page report that describes the reaction of politicians, businesses, and consumer groups to the issue as well as any laws that have been passed to regulate the use of consumer information by businesses.

LESSON 2.8
CONSUMER DECISIONS

DEFINE consumer needs and buying motives

IDENTIFY the steps in consumer decision making

CONSUMERS SATISFY NEEDS AND WANTS

Every time you go to the store, you go through a decision-making process based on your needs and wants. What do you want to buy? Do you really need it? Can you afford it? What if it isn't really what you expected? Depending on the importance of the need or want and the amount of money you have available, the decision may be easy or difficult. In order to offer marketing mixes that will satisfy their customers, marketers need to understand consumer needs as well as how consumers make decisions.

Wants and needs provide the basis for buying behavior. A **want** is an unfulfilled desire. Consumers want to wear the latest fashions, ride in the newest models of automobiles, and own the latest electronic gadgets. A **need** is anything you require to live. You need healthy food, shelter, education, and clean air and water.

ON THE $CENE

Ali and his friends gathered outside of school on Friday afternoon. It had been a busy week and they were all ready to relax. But what should they do? Would it be more fun to go to a movie or rent a DVD? The pro hockey team's first exhibition game was scheduled for this evening and the Youth League had discount tickets. Ali had just purchased the new NHL video game and was anxious to try it out. All of the choices required a commitment of time and some money. Each person had his or her own idea of what would be the best choice, but the group didn't have much time to decide. How can one decision satisfy everyone?

Abraham Maslow developed a widely accepted theory on human motivation. Maslow's *hierarchy of needs* identifies five areas that guide behavior—physiological, security, social, esteem, and self-actualization. Maslow suggested that people progress through the levels of need. The higher levels do not influence behavior until the lower levels are reasonably satisfied. However, if people are not hungry, and feel safe, secure, and accepted, they will be motivated more by esteem and self-actualization needs.

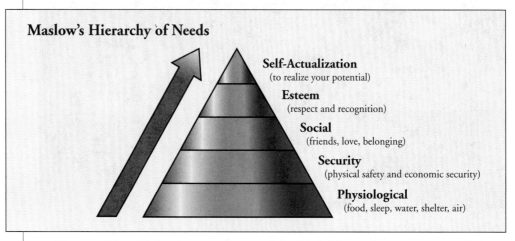

Maslow's Hierarchy of Needs

Self-Actualization (to realize your potential)

Esteem (respect and recognition)

Social (friends, love, belonging)

Security (physical safety and economic security)

Physiological (food, sleep, water, shelter, air)

You can identify businesses that use Maslow's hierarchy to promote their products. Tire manufacturers and home security businesses often appeal to safety and security needs. Insurance companies and financial planners emphasize economic security. The Army appealed to esteem and self-actualization with its call to "be all that you can be."

MOTIVATION TO BUY

Consumers often express their wants and needs by identifying the products and services they would like to purchase. However, the products and services represent ways to satisfy the needs. You might say, "I need a hair dryer." However, the hair dryer provides a way to quickly manage and style your hair. You might say, "I need a driver's license." In reality, obtaining your license gives you the freedom to travel without asking someone else to provide transportation and it provides a feeling of power and control.

The decision to purchase products and services are guided by buying motives. **Buying motives** are the reasons that you buy. The three categories of buying motives that drive consumers to purchase products or services are emotional, rational, and loyalty.

Emotional motives are reasons to purchase based on feelings, beliefs, or attitudes. Emotions are very strong and influence your actions and purchases in many situations. You buy greeting cards and gifts out of love and friendship. You go to amusement parks because of the excitement and thrills of the rides and games. Fear, anxiety, and concern may influence us to search for products and services, such as insurance, that address those emotions.

Rational motives are reasons to buy based on facts or logic. You may want the most durable pair of athletic shoes or the most economical airline ticket. Automobile dealers that emphasize the performance ratings or fuel efficiency of their brands are appealing to rational buying motives.

GENDER DIFFERENCES ONLINE Understanding similarities and difference among consumer groups allows businesses to tailor their marketing mixes to specific needs and interests. A study by Jupiter Communications found that teenage males and females surf the Web in different ways.

Males	Females
Make surfing decisions based on their interests	Look for familiar brands
Focus on technology, entertainment, and ways to fill their time	Want to interact with others who share their interests
Spend more time surfing and visit more sites	Are goal oriented in surfing
	Have a preference for off-line products and brands

THINK CRITICALLY If you were marketing to teenage males online, what products would you feature and what needs would you emphasize? How would you approach online marketing differently for teenage females?

Loyalty motives are based on satisfying relationships. If you have had several positive experiences with a particular business or brand, you are likely to continue to use them without a great deal of thought. People are influenced by their affiliation with groups and organizations or their identification with a popular person. Companies that use actors, athletes, or other famous people as spokespeople for their products are appealing to loyalty motives.

CHECKPOINT

What is the difference between needs and wants?

_____

_____

CONSUMER DECISION-MAKING PROCESS

Purchasing a product is a lot like eating and breathing. You do it so often, you don't think much about it. But you go through a specific procedure every time you decide whether to buy something or not. After deciding to make a purchase, you must choose the business and brand you will buy.

For some products you purchase regularly, you may have a particular store you will typically visit and a brand you prefer. In other cases, you may not have a preference, knowing that several stores or brands will meet your needs. If you are shopping for a new product, or if the possible purchase is quite expensive, you may be very careful in gathering information and comparing alternatives before making the final selection.

The decision processes and actions of consumers as they buy and use services and products is called **buying behavior**. Marketers want to understand their customers' buying behavior so they can assist them in making the best possible decisions that will offer the most need satisfaction.

Consumers go through five steps when making a purchase decision. They move from problem recognition, to information search, to alternative evaluation, to purchase, and finally to post-purchase evaluation.

Problem Recognition   First the consumer must recognize a need, desire, or problem. You won't be interested in purchasing a backpack until the school year is about to begin and you think about having to carry books and supplies all day long. Once you recognize the need, you begin to consider ways to satisfy it, often with the purchase of a product or service.

Information Search   Next, the consumer gathers information about alternative solutions. You will consider how you satisfied the need in the past. You may ask friends or experts for advice or gather information from magazines, newspapers, or the Internet. The information is designed to provide several choices of products and services to solve the problem.

Evaluation of Alternatives   Consumers use the information they gather to evaluate their choices. The goal is to determine which alternative is the best. This may mean making trade-offs between price and various options. Your evaluation may be rational, emotional, or based on loyalty.

Purchase Decision   If a suitable choice is available and affordable, the consumer will make a selection and complete the purchase. If no choice seems appropriate, the purchase may be delayed or you may decide the need isn't strong enough to warrant making an undesirable choice.

Post-purchase Evaluation   At this point the consumer uses the purchase and decides if it met the need or solved the problem. If you are satisfied with your choice, you will probably make the same decision the next time and may even recommend the product to your family and friends. If you are dissatisfied, you will not buy the product again and may decide to return it to the business for a refund. You will usually tell others about an unsatisfactory experience as well.

Even though it is not always apparent, consumers follow the five steps when they make purchase decisions. In some cases, the steps are completed very quickly, even in a matter of minutes. At other times, it may take weeks and even months to select a college, buy a home, or make other risky or expensive purchases. Satisfied customers will skip quickly through the first several steps when they have a need and buy the same product over and over.

CHECKPOINT

List the five steps in the consumer decision-making process.

THINK CRITICALLY

1. How does an understanding of consumer behavior help marketers make better decisions about a marketing strategy?

They know how consumers react to different products

2. Why would consumers use emotional or loyalty motives rather than rational motives when purchasing a product?

To market their products the best they can.

3. Under what circumstances would a consumer make a decision to buy a product even if it appeared the product would not offer full satisfaction?

because they absolutely need it.

MAKE CONNECTIONS

4. **RESEARCH** Prepare a list of three products and services that many people purchase ranging from inexpensive to expensive. Survey ten people to determine the reasons they purchase each of the products or services. Then classify each reason as an emotional, rational, or loyalty motive. Summarize and present your results in a table or chart.

5. **PSYCHOLOGY** Use a word-processing or computer graphics program to draw a pyramid and label it to represent the five levels of Maslow's hierarchy of needs. For each level, list needs that you think match the level. Then identify at least three products or services that appeal to the needs at that level.

LESSON 2.4
BUSINESS-TO-BUSINESS

GOALS

DESCRIBE the types of business customers and products

DISCUSS procedures for business-to-business marketing

BUSINESSES AS CUSTOMERS

Business markets are the companies and organizations that purchase products for the operation of a business or the completion of a business activity. Business markets include producers, manufacturers, retail businesses, nonprofit organizations, government offices and agencies, schools, and other types of groups that provide products or services for consumption by others. Business markets make purchase decisions on the basis of what is needed to effectively operate the business, to meet the needs of employees and customers of the business, and to produce the products and services of the business.

Do you think marketing to businesses and organizations should be done in a different way than marketing to final consumers? In some cases busi-

ON THE $CENE

Janice enjoys being a professional salesperson. She worked in retail stores while she was in high school and college. For five years since completing her marketing degree, she has been successful working for a national retail chain selling personal computers to individuals and families. The chain has decided to begin selling computers to businesses. The top salespeople are being selected for sales teams that will work with large businesses to determine their computer needs. The company has asked Janice to join one of the teams. How do you think selling computers to businesses as a part of a sales team will differ from selling computers to individuals and families in a retail store?

nesses purchase the same products as final consumers. However, businesses usually purchase products—such as computers, telephones, automobiles—in much larger quantities. In other cases, businesses purchase products seldom purchased by final consumers, such as jet fuel, a factory, and a product scanning system for inventory control.

Even though the products may differ, the basic marketing process does not. Business marketers must identify the target markets to be served, determine their characteristics and needs, and develop a marketing mix that meets their business customers' needs better than their competition. Just as all consumers are not the same, businesses also have important differences that require different marketing strategies.

CATEGORIES OF BUSINESSES

One way of classifying business consumers is by the type of organization. The major categories of businesses are producers, resellers, service businesses, government, and nonprofit organizations.

Producers More than six million businesses in the United States produce products for sale to final consumers and other businesses. They can be very small businesses that employ only a few people or companies as large as Microsoft or Procter and Gamble that each employ several hundred thousand people worldwide.

Resellers Wholesale and retail businesses are a part of the product distribution system connecting producers with consumers. They purchase products for resale. As a part of that process they may maintain distribution and storage services, promote products through advertising and personal selling, extend credit to consumers, and complete a variety of other marketing activities designed to meet customer needs. More than three million businesses operate as resellers in the U.S. economy.

Service Businesses More than seven million service businesses were operating in 2000. That number is growing faster than any other category of businesses. Services are activities provided directly to the customer by a business. Services cover a broad range of activities including insurance, transportation, accounting, cleaning, repair, and many others.

Government Federal, state, and local government offices and agencies provide services to citizens including individuals and businesses. They also develop and enforce laws and regulations. The U.S. government is the largest single customer in the world. From a supplier's viewpoint, the government is made up of thousands of separate customers with very different needs.

Nonprofit Organizations Many organizations have specific goals or clients that they are organized to serve, and providing that service is the reason they exist. While they need an adequate budget to operate, profit is not the primary motive for their existence. Common examples of these organizations are schools, museums, churches, shelters, community centers, colleges and universities, and professional organizations.

Each of the types of businesses described is a prospective customer for other businesses. Whether businesses sell to final consumers, businesses, or a combination, the business needs to carefully study prospective customers and their needs, select the most appropriate target markets, and develop a specific marketing mix for each market.

TYPES OF BUSINESS PURCHASES

Recognizing the types of purchases businesses make will help you understand the business market. There are five categories of products used by businesses. These are capital equipment, operating equipment, raw materials, component parts, and supplies.

Capital Equipment The land, buildings, and major pieces of equipment are usually the most expensive products purchased by a business. They are also the most important. They must meet the specific needs of the business so it operates effectively. Often they are individually designed and can be very expensive. They usually are purchased after careful planning and are expected to be used by the business for many years.

Operating Equipment Smaller, less expensive equipment used in the operation of the business or in the production and sale of products and services is known as operating equipment. Examples of operating equipment are tools, small machines, and furniture. They usually have a shorter life than capital equipment and must be replaced from time to time.

Raw Materials Producers and manufacturers buy many products that are incorporated into the products they make. Raw materials are unprocessed products used as basic materials for the products to be produced. Lumber, steel, plastic, grain, fabric, and cement are just a few examples of raw materials. Purchasers of raw materials must have an adequate supply and a standard quality of the raw materials they use to produce their products. The price of the raw materials also is important, because the cost has a big influence on what the company charges for its finished products.

Component Parts Component parts also are incorporated into the products that a business makes. However, component parts have been processed either partially or totally by another company. For example, a computer manufacturer will buy computer chips from one company and assembled hard drives from another. Those parts are then integrated as a part of the final computer assembly.

Supplies The products and materials consumed in the operation of the business are supplies. The supplies needed are often unique to a type of business but common examples are cleaning supplies, pencils, pens, light bulbs, and printer cartridges. Some supplies are purchased and used in very small quantities and are quite inexpensive. Others, such as fuel, electricity, or water may be needed in large quantities and are a major expense for the company.

CHECKPOINT

What are the five types of products used by businesses?

_____

_____

MARKETING TO BUSINESSES

Businesses that sell to other businesses use the same general marketing procedures as those that market to final consumers. They must develop a marketing strategy and complete each of the seven marketing functions. Effective marketing relies on understanding unique characteristics of business customers and the way they make purchase decisions.

CHARACTERISTICS OF BUSINESS CUSTOMERS

Some characteristics of business customers influence the specific marketing procedures a business will use. The types of purchases their customers make, the volume purchased, and the relationship they have with their customers all influence the way businesses market their products and services.

Types of Purchases Businesses make purchases to be used directly or indirectly in meeting the needs of final consumers. The types and quantities of products and services demanded by the business are derived from the level of demand of their customers. Businesses that produce or resell similar products and services usually have common purchasing needs. Consider two construction companies that build homes. Each company will purchase many of the same types of equipment and materials.

Purchase Volume The number of business customers that make up a market for a particular type of product usually is smaller than the number of final consumers who will purchase a product. However, the business customers usually purchase a much larger quantity of each product.

Buyer/Seller Relationship In business-to-business selling the seller often is in direct contact with the customer. This results in closer buyer/seller relationships, better understanding of needs, and effective customer service.

JUST THE FACTS

You probably think of the Central Intelligence Agency (CIA) as the federal agency that spies on other countries. However, the CIA is a large data collection and analysis organization. While its primary purpose is providing intelligence information for security purposes, it is a valuable resource for businesses involved in international business. The CIA publishes the annual *World Fact Book* that provides a comprehensive report of information it collects on countries from all over the world. Up-to-date information is provided on each country's geography, people, government, economy, transportation, communications, and military. It also includes maps and information on issues that might affect international relations.

THINK CRITICALLY How might a business use information from the CIA *World Fact Book*?

WORKSHOP

List the five types of businesses. Use a business directory or telephone directory for your community to identify two businesses or organizations that fit each type. List three products or services you think the businesses would need to purchase. Use the directory to locate a possible supplier of each product. Prepare a table that presents your results.

BUSINESS PURCHASES

While the decisions of individual consumers often are guided by emotion, business purchasing usually is very rational. A purchase is not made unless the product or service is useful in the operation of the business or can be resold to customers. The product or service purchased will be the one that best meets the needs of the business at a reasonable price. If the purchase does not improve the business or cannot be sold to customers, the business will not be successful. If the business pays too much for a purchase, it will make it difficult to make a profit. Therefore, business purchasing is done very carefully.

Purchasing Specialists Purchasing in businesses occurs continuously and may involve thousands, even millions, of dollars each day. Many of the products purchased are unique and very complex. The purchasing process involves arranging delivery and payment schedules. Often lengthy and complex contracts are prepared between the buyer and seller. Because the process is so important and complicated, many businesses have departments and personnel that specialize in purchasing. Job titles for people involved in purchasing include buyers, product managers, merchandise managers, and purchasing agents.

Evaluating Purchases When a purchase is made, the buyer determines if the product meets the needs as closely as possible. That also is true for business customers. Businesses normally develop very detailed specifications for products. They use those specifications in evaluating purchases. The needs of the business's customers also are considered in the evaluation process. When the purchases meet the buyer's needs, the buyer usually will continue to purchase from the same supplier unless needs change or the supplier is no longer able to meet the purchasing requirements of the buyer.

Businesses continually evaluate purchasing procedures and the products and services purchased to improve their purchasing performance. One of the management methods companies use to improve purchasing is known as just-in-time (JIT) purchasing. With JIT purchasing, a company develops a relationship with its suppliers to keep inventory levels low and to re-supply inventory on an as-needed basis.

CHECKPOINT

How do purchases made by business customers differ from the purchases of final consumers?

_____

_____

THINK CRITICALLY

1. In what ways are business customers similar to and different from final consumers?

_____

_____

_____

_____

2. Why are service businesses the fastest-growing category of business customers?

_____

_____

_____

3. Develop examples of each of the five categories of business products.

_____

_____

_____

_____

4. Why might businesses continue to purchase products such as raw materials or component parts from the same supplier?

_____

_____

_____

MAKE CONNECTIONS

5. ACCOUNTING Businesses follow specific procedures to purchase products and services. Usually a specific document, called a _purchase order_, is completed and sent to the seller. Using an accounting text or the Internet locate an example of a business purchase order. Photocopy the form or recreate the form on a computer using word-processing software. Assume you are a purchasing agent for a business. Fill in the form to order five desktop computers for your company. Use the Internet or library resources to locate a supplier and the necessary purchase information. Use spreadsheet software to perform the calculations.

6. GOVERNMENT Local, state, and federal governments are an important part of business-to-business marketing and business-to-consumer marketing. Government agencies are both suppliers of products and services and customers for the products and services supplied by other businesses. Use the Internet to find examples of each of the following: (1) products and services offered for sale by a government agency to businesses, (2) products and services offered for sale by a government agency to individual consumers, (3) products and services purchased by a government agency for use in its operations.

REVIEW

CHAPTER SUMMARY

LESSON 2.1 Marketing Strategy

A. A company's plan that identifies how it will use marketing to achieve its goals is known as a marketing strategy.

B. Businesses using the marketing concept identify and select a target market and then develop a marketing mix to satisfy its needs.

LESSON 2.2 Marketing Research

A. Businesses have a much greater chance of success if they carefully determine the information they need to plan and market products.

B. If a business needs information that is not currently available, the company will need to use marketing research to gather the information.

LESSON 2.3 Consumer Decisions

A. Marketers must understand consumer needs and how consumers make decisions in order to offer marketing mixes that will satisfy their customers.

B. Consumers go through five steps when making a purchase decision. They move from problem recognition, to information search, to alternative evaluation, to purchase, and finally to post-purchase evaluation.

LESSON 2.4 Business-to-Business

A. Business markets include producers, manufacturers, retail businesses, nonprofit organizations, government agencies and other organizations that provide products or services for consumption by others.

B. While the decisions of individual consumers often are guided by emotion, business purchasing usually is very rational.

VOCABULARY BUILDER

Choose the term that best fits the definition. Write the letter of the answer in the space provided. Some terms may not be used.

_g_ **1.** Company plan that identifies how it will use marketing to achieve its goals

_e_ **2.** Prospective customers a company wants to serve

_i_ **3.** Segment of a market in which customers have similar characteristics and needs

_j_ **4.** An unfulfilled desire

_h_ **5.** Anything you require to live

_c_ **6.** Reasons that you buy

_g_ **7.** Blending of four marketing elements—product, distribution, price, and promotion

_b_ **8.** Decision processes and actions of consumers as they buy and use services and products

_f_ **9.** Companies and organizations that purchase products for the operation of a business or the completion of a business activity

a. business markets
b. buying behavior
c. buying motives
d. market
e. marketing mix
f. marketing research
g. marketing strategy
h. need
i. target market
j. want

POINT YOUR BROWSER

b2000.swep.com

REVIEW CONCEPTS

10. What are the two steps in developing a marketing strategy?

- Plan of attack
- ways your going to market

11. Identify the four elements of a marketing mix.

Product, distribution, promotion, pricing.

12. What customer information does a business need in order to select a target market?

A group of people with similar needs + wants.

13. What are three methods businesses use to collect data in marketing research?

- Surveys
- Observations
- experiments

14. What is the difference between an emotional and a rational buying motive?

emotional = feelings or beliefs
rational = facts or logic

15. Describe the process consumers go through to make a purchase decision.

Problem solving, info gathering, evaluation of alternatives, purchase decisions, post person evaluation.

16. Identify several categories of business customers.

producers, resellers, service businesses, government, non-profit organizations

17. Why do businesses frequently use purchasing specialists?

_____

_____

_____

APPLY WHAT YOU LEARNED

18. Provide examples of two unique target markets for a computer manufacturer.

_____

_____

_____

19. What is the highest level of Maslow's hierarchy of needs? Name several examples of products and services that appeal to this need.

_____

_____

_____

20. How does the consumer decision-making process differ for a product purchased regularly and one that is being purchased for the first time?

_____

_____

_____

21. Why would a business use a survey to gather marketing research information rather than conducting an experiment?

_____

_____

_____

22. How do you think the needs and purchase procedures of a government agency might be different from those of a private business?

_____

_____

_____

23. Why do businesses often continue to use the same supplier to buy products and services? What might cause them to change suppliers?

_____

_____

_____

_____

MAKE CONNECTIONS

24. RESEARCH Outline the procedure a marketing researcher would follow in determining the most effective brand name for a new product. Try to organize the procedure within the five steps of the scientific decision-making process. Does it appear that the scientific decision-making process is an effective procedure for marketing research? Why or why not? Prepare your outline and answer using word-processing software.

25. BUSINESS MATH A purchasing agent has been given the following information to complete an order. Enter the information into a spreadsheet. Determine the cost of each product and the total cost of the order.

Product	Price/Unit	Numbered Ordered	Cost
Plastic tubes	$1.20/doz.	88 doz.	_____
Glassware	$33.50/case	22 cases	_____
Paper	$4.65/ream	350 reams	_____
Blank CDs	$18.00/hundred	6,000 CDs	_____
Manuals	$3.80 each	135 units	_____
		Total Cost	_____

26. ART Select a product to analyze. Determine the marketing mix that is being used by the company for the product. Using poster board or a graphics programs on a computer, create a picture or collage that illustrates each of the elements of the marketing mix. Present your graphic in class.

27. TECHNOLOGY The Internet is used as a way for businesses to conduct customer surveys as a part of their marketing research. Find an example of an online marketing research survey. Print a copy of the survey. Review the survey to determine the type of information the business is collecting. Discuss with your class how you think the information collected can be used by the business to improve marketing decisions.

_____

_____

_____

_____

CHAPTER 3

PLAN PRODUCTS AND SERVICES

LESSONS

3.1 THE PRODUCT

3.2 PRODUCT PLANNING

3.3 PRODUCT LIFE CYCLES

3.4 EFFECTIVE SERVICES

CAREERS IN
MARKETING

SPRINT CORPORATION

The Brown Telephone Company was formed in 1899 to provide local telephone service to communities in Kansas. It became Sprint Corporation in 1992. Over the years, the company has focused on being a technology leader. Sprint was a pioneer in the use of fiber-optic cable and digital switches.

Sprint's Asia Business Development Manager is responsible for product expansion in assigned countries. The manager gathers competitive intelligence, checks the economic, technological, and operational feasibility of ideas, and develops partnership relationships with other businesses.

The Manager needs a college degree in business, management, or engineering and five years' experience in the telecommunications industry. Financial and business analysis skills are essential as well as leadership, entrepreneurial, and negotiation skills. The manager needs to be fluent in English and the languages of the assigned countries.

THINK CRITICALLY

1. How do you think Sprint has been able to maintain its success?
2. What would you find interesting and challenging about the position of Business Development Manager?

The Chapter 3 video for this module introduces the concepts in this chapter.

PROJECT
Develop Products

PROJECT OBJECTIVES

- Identify how customer needs influence product development
- Describe sources of new product ideas
- Analyze a new product to determine factors influencing its success
- Identify ways to provide effective services

GETTING STARTED

Read through the Project Process below. Make a list of materials and information you will need. Decide how you will get the needed materials or information.

PROJECT PROCESS

Part 1 LESSON 3.1 Work in small groups to develop a questionnaire. The purpose of the questionnaire is to obtain feedback from customers on a company's products. Prepare at least 10 questions that help to determine what the customer likes and dislikes about the product, how it compares to other products, and what improvements they would like to see.

Part 2 LESSON 3.2 In your groups, brainstorm ideas for improvements to existing products. Then brainstorm ideas for brand new products. After you complete the lists, share them with the other groups in your class. As a class, use a ranking procedure to identify the five product improvement ideas and five new product ideas you think have the greatest chance for success.

Part 3 LESSON 3.3 Use the Internet to identify a new consumer product that has been introduced within the past two years. List two competitive brands for the new product. List the similarities and differences among the three brands. Identify advantages you think the new product offers to consumers compared to existing brands.

Part 4 LESSON 3.4 Identify a service provided by a business in your community that you think is provided very well. Then identify another service that you think is not provided well. Compare the two and develop a list of factors that justify your decision about the quality of the services.

CHAPTER REVIEW

Project Wrap-up Discuss product and service development with other class members. Prepare a list of recommendations you would provide to companies to help them develop successful new products and services.

LESSON 3.1
THE PRODUCT

GOALS

DESCRIBE business and customer views of products

IDENTIFY the components of the product mix element

WHAT IS A PRODUCT?

A product or service is usually the focus of exchange activities between customers and businesses. It is the marketing mix element that most businesses consider first when planning a marketing strategy. It also is the first consideration for consumers as they determine what they plan to purchase.

A product is all the attributes, both tangible and intangible, that a business offers to customers in exchange for their money. Businesses produce products and services they think customers will want to buy in order to make a profit. Customers exchange money with businesses in order to obtain the products and services they want. Businesses and consumers have very different views of this important mix element.

ON THE $CENE

The Geofase Company is a small manufacturer of specialty athletic footwear. It makes and sells footwear for wrestlers, gymnasts, fencers, and swimmers. Other athletic shoe manufacturers are selling their products to the general public as "designer" footwear by changing designs, fabrics, and colors. Designer shoes often sell for a much higher price than traditional athletic shoes. The Geofase Company wonders if it can compete in this new market. It will cost money to develop and produce the new designs. But the higher prices and broader market could result in greater profits for the company. What information do you think Geofase needs to make the decision? What factors will influence its success with the new products?

BUSINESS AND CONSUMER VIEW OF PRODUCTS

Businesses tend to focus on the physical characteristics of the products they sell. They use people and resources to produce products. They want to produce a good product that will be competitive and result in a profit when sold. They are concerned about how their product differs from the products of competitors, how they can improve it, or how to produce it more efficiently.

Consumers are most concerned about their wants and needs. They view products as solutions. A CD or movie provides entertainment. A new clothing purchase enhances self-image. Consumers are seldom concerned about how the product is produced or whether the seller will make a profit.

A good definition of **product** is anything offered to a market by the business to satisfy needs. That definition includes the business view of product—anything offered to a market by a business. It also includes the consumer view of a product—anything that satisfies needs. Businesses will be able to make a profit if they consider customer needs as they develop products.

PRODUCT DECISIONS

Some customer needs are obvious and easy to identify, while others are difficult for businesses to recognize. Because of the variety of customer needs, the uses for products, and the number of competing companies producing and selling products, companies must plan products carefully. If companies produce the wrong products in the wrong quantities without the features and services customers need, they will have invested a great deal of time and money with no chance to sell the products at a profit. They will quickly lose out to competitors who make better product decisions.

Product planning for businesses involves deciding which customers to serve, determining their needs, and developing a satisfying product for that market. Because many companies compete to sell their products to the same customers, the business will need to offer a product that is different from—and better than—other choices available to the customer. It will need to be affordable and available at a time and location convenient for the customer. It should be accompanied by information that will help the customer understand why the company's product is the best choice.

> **did you KNOW?**
>
> During the period of 1986 to 1996, the number of new products introduced in supermarkets grew from 12,500 to 26,000 per year. However, only about 8 percent were truly new. The rest were improvements to existing products.

BUSINESS MATH CONNECTION

Businesses calculate the *breakeven point* to determine the number of products they need to sell to cover their costs before they start making a profit. One product has fixed costs of $83,500, no matter how many units are produced. It has variable costs of $10.50 for each unit produced. The company plans to sell the product for $54.00. How many products will it have to produce and sell to break even?

SOLUTION

To find the breakeven point, divide the fixed costs by the selling price minus the variable costs. The breakeven point is 1,920 units.

Fixed costs ÷ (Selling price − Variable costs) = Breakeven point

$83,500 ÷ ($54.00 − $10.50) = 1,919.54, or 1,920 units

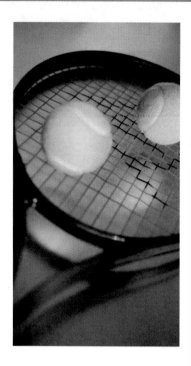

LEVELS OF PRODUCTS

In planning a product, businesses consider three levels—a basic product, an enhanced product, and an extended product. The *basic product* is the physical product in its simplest form. The basic product of one company will usually be very much like that of its competitors. The basic product must clearly meet a consumer need. An example is a tennis racket. Many companies produce and sell them, and it is obvious what the product is and what it is used for.

To make their product different from competitors' products and to meet specific needs of consumers, companies develop an enhanced product. An *enhanced product* adds features and options to the basic product. The tennis racket can be constructed of different materials, sizes, and weights. It may be strung or unstrung and offer choices of grips.

An *extended product* includes additional features that are not part of the physical product but increase its usability. Examples are customer service, guarantees, and information on effective use, and additional products that improve the use of the product. People who purchase a tennis racket may need bags, balls, wristbands, or instructional videos. The choices allow customers to get just the right products to meet specialized needs.

CHECKPOINT

What are the levels of product a company considers when planning a new product?

_____

_____

COMPONENTS OF THE PRODUCT

Decisions about what to offer customers will potentially differ each time product planning decisions are made. They are based on what the customer wants and what the company is able to offer. In some cases, consumers in the target market want just the basic product. At other times they want a number of product features, services, and support in using the product.

Basic Product The basic product is the first factor considered in deciding whether or not to purchase. If the basic product is not viewed as need satisfying, the consumer will not consider it as a reasonable alternative. Services also can be the basic product in a marketing mix. Hair stylists, catering services, and accounting businesses all offer a basic service.

Features After the basic product or service is identified, businesses can add features. Most basic products are sold with a number of additional features. **Features** are added to improve the basic product. Consider all of the possible features on a product as simple as a wristwatch. It can display the month and day as well as times in multiple time zones. Some watches have a built-in calculator or stop-watch function. Watches can be waterproof and shockproof. The cases and bands are made from various materials designed to make them more attractive, lightweight, or durable.

Packaging The primary purpose of *packaging* is to provide protection and security for the product during distribution. The package also can provide information about the product. Packages are used to promote the product through the use of color, shape, images, and information. Packaging can even make the product more useful for the consumer as with children's drink boxes with attached straws and window cleaners that attach to a garden hose.

Support Services If you purchase a computer, cellular telephone, or home entertainment system today, the salesperson will probably offer you a maintenance contract. The *maintenance contract* is a support service that will pay for repair work if the product fails to operate properly. Many times the services provided with a product make the product easier to use. Customers will want to purchase support services if they are concerned they will be unable to assemble or operate a product or if they want assistance in its use.

Brand and Image A **brand** is a name, symbol, word, or design that identifies a product, service, or company. A brand is very important to a company because it provides a unique identification for it and its offerings. There may be a few items that you will refuse to purchase unless you can find the brand you want. With other products you aren't even aware of the brand or are satisfied with one of several available brands.

One of the major reasons for brand loyalty is the image of the brand. The brand's **image** is a unique, memorable quality of a brand. Some brands have an image of quality, others of low price, and still others as innovative. Brand image must match the important needs of the consumer to be effective.

INCREASE IN PRODUCT VALUE

When customers purchase products or services, they want to receive a good value. If the product is poorly constructed, will not work properly, or may wear out quickly, consumers may be unwilling to purchase it. Companies offer guarantees or warranties as insurance that the product will be repaired or replaced if there are problems. If a customer thinks a company will stand behind its products, they are more likely to purchase from that company.

Another way to add value is to increase the number of ways a product can be used. A classic example of expanding markets through new product uses is baking soda. Very few consumers bake their own bread today, so a baking soda manufacturer saw sales declining. The company conducted a consumer behavior study and found that consumers use baking soda for many other purposes. Some use it to freshen refrigerators, garbage disposals, and litter boxes for pets. Others use it to brush their teeth. Through promoting those and other uses, the company increased its sales dramatically.

WORKSHOP

Work in small groups to analyze three different products—one that costs less than $5, one that costs between $25 and $100, and one that costs more than $10,000. Prepare a chart for each product that identifies the basic product, features and options, related services, packaging features, brand and image, guarantees or warranties, and uses of the product. Compare your charts with those of other groups.

CHECKPOINT

What are the components of the product mix element?

_____

_____

THINK CRITICALLY

1. Why is the product component usually the first to be considered by companies when they are developing a marketing mix?

It is the first because you can't do the others before you do that.

2. Why is an extended product important for some products but not for others?

It can either make it better or worse

3. Why would a company add features to a product?

To make the product better.

4. For what types of purchases would a warranty be very important? Why?

For stuff that you would want to last

MAKE CONNECTIONS

5. ADVERTISING Use word-processing software to write an advertisement for a new brand of breakfast cereal bar. The product name is "All Day Energy" and the target market is 15- to 30-year-old males and females who are active, concerned about their fitness, yet have difficulty finding time to eat a complete breakfast.

6. DEBATE Some fast-food restaurants and cereal manufacturers give small toys and games to children with a food purchase. The purpose is to have children encourage their parents to buy the company's brand. Some people suggest that this results in purchases made for the wrong reasons. Organize a debate in your class using the following statement.

Companies should not be able to use unrelated products (games and toys) as an incentive to encourage the purchase of fast food and cereal for children.

LESSON 3.2
PRODUCT PLANNING

DESCRIBE ways that marketing is involved in new product development

IDENTIFY the steps in the product planning process

THE PRODUCT PLANNING FUNCTION

How do new products get developed in a business and who is responsible? You may imagine inventors, engineers, or scientists working in laboratories. Certainly those people are actively involved in developing new product ideas. But they do not work alone. Companies that have a marketing orientation involve marketing personnel in the planning process.

One of the seven marketing functions is **product/service planning**, or assisting in the design and development of products and services that will meet the needs of prospective customers. The key parts of that definition are

ON THE $CENE

Fast-food restaurants compete with each other and with full-service restaurants, delis, and supermarkets that sell prepared or ready-to-cook meals. Fast-food businesses are constantly searching for new products that will attract new customers or bring current customers into the restaurant more frequently. The foods must be relatively low cost and meet the tastes of many people. What new food items have fast-food restaurants successfully introduced in the past few years? What items have been introduced that were not successful? What do you think were the differences between the successful and unsuccessful products? How do you think the restaurants can identify new products that will be successful?

assisting, meaning that marketers work cooperatively with others in product development, and *meet the needs*, meaning that the products of a company are designed to satisfy customers.

THE ROLE OF MARKETING

Put yourself in the position of a salesperson of a product for which the consumer does not see a need or a product that does not appear to be better than competing products. Your success depends on selling the product. You must

try to convince the customer the product is needed or that it is better than the competitors, even if it is not. That certainly is not easy and is probably not the right thing to do.

To avoid that problem, a company uses marketing as the eyes, ears, and mouth of the customer in a business. Marketing is the direct link between a business and its customers. Marketers work with customers every day, whether in selling, promotion, product distribution, marketing research, or the many other marketing activities that occur in a business. Because of that close contact, marketers are in a good position to understand customers. They know what they like and do not like, how they view competing products, and whether they are satisfied with current products.

MARKETING AND PRODUCT PLANNING

Marketers represent the consumer in the business as products are designed and developed. There are three important roles for marketers in the product development process.

Conduct Research The most important role for marketing in product development is market research. Gathering market information, studying it, and providing the results to scientists, engineers, and others involved in new product development keeps the focus on consumer needs and competition rather than the perceptions of the people involved in planning. Through research, marketers can study the competition, identify target markets, review alternative product designs and features, and analyze several product choices.

Marketing departments that are actively involved in product planning usually develop and use a *marketing information system*. It allows the information from many sources to be collected, stored, and analyzed when needed to improve new product decisions. Sales data, salesperson and customer feedback, customer requests and complaints, and other information are included in a marketing information system.

Develop the Marketing Mix A new product is a part of a marketing strategy developed to achieve specific objectives. If the company's goal is to increase its share of a specific market, it might develop a different product than if the goal is to enter a market it has never competed in before. A new company that cannot risk failure with a new product may approach product development in a very different way than an experienced and profitable company.

A marketing strategy combines decisions about a target market and an appropriate marketing mix. The actual product is only one part of the strategy. Marketers participate in developing an effective strategy by helping identify possible target markets, determining company strengths and weaknesses, evaluating market positions, and suggesting alternative marketing mixes.

Conduct Market Tests After a product and the remaining parts of the marketing mix have been designed, marketers conduct tests to determine if the new product will be successful. There are several ways to test a new marketing mix. Some companies use test markets. A *test market* is a small, representative part of the total market. Companies introduce the new product in test markets before investing in the cost of entering the entire market.

Test marketing is very expensive, so other types of market tests are used. Companies form focus groups and other consumer panels to review product ideas and marketing mix choices. There are sophisticated computer programs that allow companies to simulate the marketing of products and determine expected levels of sales and profits.

CHECKPOINT

Why is it important for marketers to be involved in new product development?

NEW PRODUCT PLANNING

Most companies follow a very careful process to identify and develop new products. The process is used to eliminate products that are not likely to be successful before the company spends too much money for production and marketing. The process also is used to make sure that the products meet an important market need, can be produced at a reasonable price, and will be competitive with other products in the market. There are six steps in the new product development process.

IDEA DEVELOPMENT

Companies need an ongoing process to create and consider ideas for new products or product improvements. It is very difficult to find ideas for products that are really new. Developing new product ideas can be a very creative process. Tools such as brainstorming, creative thinking exercises, and problem solving are used to identify product ideas for testing.

Because products are developed to meet consumer needs, gathering information from consumers may generate ideas for new products. New product ideas can be developed from problems customers are having, what they don't like about current products, or the complaints they make to the company.

IDEA SCREENING

The second step is to carefully screen all new product ideas to select those that have the greatest chance of being successful. Businesses ask specific questions to test the ideas, such as the following.

- Is there a specific market and adequate demand for the product?
- Is competition in the market favorable for the company?
- Does the company have resources to produce the product?
- Is the product legal and safe?
- Do the costs of producing and marketing the product present an opportunity for profitable sales?

STRATEGY DEVELOPMENT

After determining that the product idea seems reasonable, the business creates and tests a sample marketing strategy. In this step, research is done to clearly identify an appropriate target market and insure that customers exist with the need and money for the product. Next, several alternative marketing mixes are analyzed to determine the possible combinations of product, distribution, price, and promotion. Based on that study, the best mix is selected. It is possible that the research in this step will determine that an effective mix cannot be developed, in which case the product idea would be dropped.

FINANCIAL ANALYSIS

If research determines that a new product idea meets a market need and can be developed, the company will complete a detailed financial analysis. It will calculate costs of production and marketing, sales projections for the target market, and potential profits. Companies use computer models to help with financial analysis. The results of the analysis are matched against company goals and profit objectives to determine if the product should be developed and marketed.

International Product Leadership

Companies must be cautious in recognizing the type of competition they face as they move into international markets. Often, businesspeople and consumers alike think businesses in their own countries are their primary competitors. However, specific countries have developed reputations as leaders in producing and marketing certain categories of products. The U.S. is recognized worldwide for its entertainment and movie industries. Japan has a reputation for producing quality automobiles. Argentina exports agricultural products. France is a leading headquarters for airplane production.

THINK CRITICALLY Why do businesspeople and consumers often fail to recognize the strong competition provided by businesses from other countries?

PRODUCT DEVELOPMENT AND TESTING

Following this careful research and planning, the company develops the product. For a manufacturer, that means designing the production process, obtaining the needed equipment and materials, and training the production personnel. For very expensive or very risky products, the company may decide to develop a **prototype**, or sample, of the product. The prototype can be used to test quality and costs before moving to full-scale production.

PRODUCT INTRODUCTION

After the product has been developed, the company prepares for its full-scale introduction. All of the marketing mix elements must be planned and implemented. Cooperating companies such as wholesalers, retailers, transportation companies, and advertising agencies need to be involved. Production levels must be high enough to have an adequate supply of the product available to meet the target market needs. Marketing personnel need to be prepared for their responsibilities. All of the activities must be coordinated and controlled by managers.

The company needs to be very cautious when preparing for the product introduction. It is possible that conditions will have changed, competitors may have anticipated the new product, or consumers will not respond in exactly the way predicted. Adjustments in the marketing strategy may be needed.

CHECKPOINT

What are the six steps in the new product planning process?

THINK CRITICALLY

1. Why is there a greater likelihood of new product failure if marketers are not involved in the planning process?

because they do not have the info to make the product good.

2. Why do companies continue to develop new products if there is such a high failure rate?

because once you are bound to have a success.

3. Other than consumers, what are some other sources of new product ideas?

Some other sources are government agencies

4. What are advantages and disadvantages of using a test market for a new product?

You might end up with a failing product or a successful product.

MAKE CONNECTIONS

5. **SCIENCE** Research completed at universities and in government agencies has resulted in many new consumer products. Examples of those products include drugs to treat illnesses and diseases, improvements in computers and communications, and agricultural products. Use the Internet to identify current research that has the potential to result in new products. Prepare an oral report for your class that describes the research, the anticipated products and their uses, and the university, organization, or business that is conducting the research.

6. **BUSINESS LAW** Businesses and individuals can protect new product ideas through the use of patents and copyrights. Use library resources to research U.S. patent and copyright laws. Use a word-processing program to prepare a three-page report that describes the laws, how the laws provide protection, and the process for receiving a patent and a copyright.

LESSON 8.8
PRODUCT LIFE CYCLES

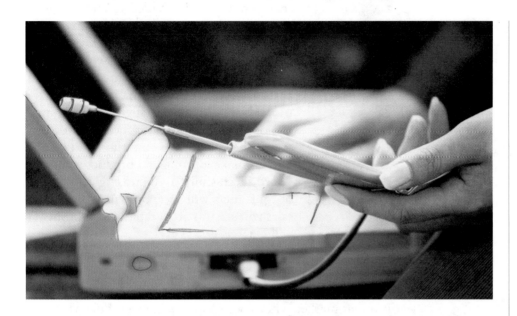

GOALS

IDENTIFY the stages of the product life cycle

DESCRIBE how life cycles help businesses plan a marketing strategy

THE PRODUCT LIFE CYCLE

Successful products move through a set of predictable stages throughout their product lives. Those stages show how profits and sales change as competition increases. The **product life cycle** describes the stages of sales and profit performance through which all brands of a product progress as a result of competition.

INTRODUCTION

In the introduction stage, a brand new product enters the market. Initially, there is only one brand of the product available for consumers to purchase.

ON THE SCENE

Daisy Dairy always had a door-to-door delivery service for milk and other dairy products. Using small, air-conditioned trucks, the company's sales-people made weekly deliveries to customers. Customers would place their next order when the weekly delivery was made. The delivery business had been very profitable for 40 years, but in the last 10 years the number of customers and size of the orders had declined, resulting in losses for the company. While three dairies originally competed for the business, Daisy Dairy was the only company left. Why do you think demand has fallen for the dairy delivery service? What recommendations would you make to Daisy Dairy about whether to continue the delivery service?

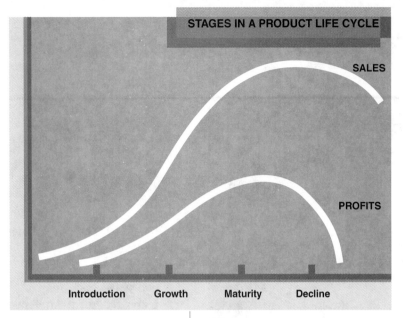

STAGES IN A PRODUCT LIFE CYCLE

SALES

PROFITS

Introduction   Growth   Maturity   Decline

The new product is quite different from, and hopefully better than, products customers are currently using. While every product has gone through the introduction stage, examples of products recently in that stage are web-ready cellular telephones, high-definition television (HDTV), and MP3 audio players that can download digital music files from the Internet. The costs of producing and marketing a new product are usually very high, resulting in a loss or very low profits for the firm initially. The company is counting on future sales to make a profit. If a product is introduced successfully, an increasing number of consumers will accept the new product, sales will start to grow rapidly, and profits will emerge.

GROWTH

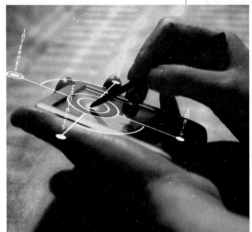

When competitors see the success of the new product, they want to get into that market. They try to copy the new product as closely as possible and make improvements. When several brands of the new product are available, the market moves into the *growth stage* of the life cycle. If customers like the new product, they begin buying it regularly and telling others about it, so the market experiences rapid sales growth. As initial costs are recovered, the industry experiences growth in profits. Examples of products that have been in the growth stage recently are digital video cameras, personal digital assistants (PDAs), and sports utility vehicles (SUVs).

MATURITY

As the market for a new product moves through the growth stage, the product is purchased by many more customers and becomes very profitable. That results in many companies in the market selling their own brand of the product. In the *maturity stage*, the product has many competing brands with very similar features. Customers have a hard time identifying differences among the brands and so have much less brand loyalty. Competition gets very intense as businesses compete for the same customers with very similar products. Products in the maturity stage include automobiles, desktop computers, cereal, toothpaste, fast food, and many others.

DECLINE

Although many products stay in the maturity stage of the life cycle for many years, sooner or later products move into a decline stage. The *decline stage* occurs when a new product is introduced that is much better or easier to use, and customers switch from the old product to the new product. As more customers are attracted to the new product, companies selling the old product see declines in profits and sales. The companies may not be able to improve the older products enough to compete with the new products, so they drop them when declining profits no longer support their existence. Examples of products that have moved through the decline stage are push lawnmowers and three-speed bicycles.

How do sales and profits change in the stages of a product life cycle?

_____

_____

_____

MARKETING ACROSS THE LIFE CYCLE

The marketing strategy needs to be adjusted at each stage of the product life cycle. The competition, target markets, and marketing mixes may change at each stage. The following suggestions describe how companies change their approach to marketing at each life cycle stage.

INTRODUCE A NEW PRODUCT

When a company introduces a new product, it needs to inform prospective customers about the product and its uses. Customers are using other products, so the company must show customers how the new product is better. Initially, only a few customers buy the product. Their experience determines whether other people want to buy it. Major marketing activities are distribution and promotion. Because the product is new, prices are likely to be high.

MANAGE PRODUCT GROWTH

In the growth stage, new companies enter the market. Each company is trying to attract customers to its brand. Companies try to improve their brands by adding features, options, and services. They also add to their channels of distribution to make the product more readily available to the growing number of customers in the market. Promotion emphasizes differences among the brands and is directed to the specific target markets the company wants to satisfy. Prices may start to decline, although customers may pay more for preferred brands or for unique features and special services. Profits are likely to increase for a time as companies sell larger quantities of products. Over time, additional marketing costs begin to reduce profits for many companies.

MOVE THROUGH MATURITY

In maturity, there are fewer new customers. Companies increase competition to gain a greater market share. Because there are so many customers, each business has to distribute the product widely, which adds to its costs. Because customers have many choices and see few differences among brands, companies spend a lot

WORKSHOP

Review magazines and newspapers to identify new products that have been introduced recently. For each product, identify the target market, competing products, and the important marketing mix elements described. Based on the information, decide which life cycle stage the product fits. Discuss your decision.

NET CHATS YIELD CONSUMER INFORMATION Companies have a new tool for keeping up with consumer ideas and opinions. Online chat rooms and bulletin boards on the Internet are places where groups with common interests meet to talk with each other about their experiences and opinions. Businesses can tap into those conversations to gain valuable insights that help them improve current products and develop new offerings. Hallmark Cards developed an "Idea Exchange" web site to hold online conversations with 200 selected consumers. Hallmark employees usually let the discussion develop around any topics the consumers choose. From time-to-time, the company asks chat room participants to answer questions or discuss how they use Hallmark products.

THINK CRITICALLY How can a chat room provide better information than a more traditional method such as a focus group? Why might a consumer choose to participate in a company-sponsored Internet chat room?

on promotion. They also reduce prices by offering sales, coupons, and rebates. Sales may increase for a time using these methods, but profits usually fall. One way businesses respond to the maturity stage is to look for new markets. Businesses often begin to move into international markets.

AVOID DECLINE

When a company sees sales and profits declining in the market, immediate changes must be made. If the declines continue it usually means that customers no longer value the product and are looking for newer and better alternatives. Some companies have been able to move old products out of the decline stage by finding new uses for them. For example, baby oil is now being used as a suntan product. If companies cannot save a product from the decline stage, they will attempt to sell their remaining inventory to the customers who still prefer it.

USE A MARKETING ORIENTATION

Companies that use a marketing orientation are in a better position to adjust to each life cycle stage. Those companies study their customers. They recognize when customer needs are not being satisfied and how customers view competitive products. Marketing-oriented companies also study the economy and the competition so they can predict when competition is increasing and are more aware if a competitor is planning a new product introduction.

How does marketing in the growth stage of a life cycle differ from marketing in the maturity stage?

_____

_____

THINK CRITICALLY

1. Why does the introductory stage of a product life cycle present difficult marketing challenges?

It can result in a loss or very low profits.

2. How can profits begin to decline in the maturity stage even while sales may still be increasing?

because copycats begin to come on the stage

3. Why is promotion important at the maturity stage of the life cycle?

To make sure your product is the best known.

4. Why do companies often wait until late in the maturity stage or even until the decline stage to look for new markets in which to sell their products?

because you never know when you could rebound.

MAKE CONNECTIONS

5. **HISTORY** Identify a major national or international company that has operated for more than 50 years. Use the Internet or other information sources to study the company. Determine how the products produced and marketed have changed over the life of the company. Identify other companies that competed with the business during its history that have gone out of business and others that have become competitors recently. Use a computer graphics program to develop a timeline that illustrates the information you collected. Present your timeline in class.

6. **BUSINESS** Work in a team with other students. Write the name of each of the four stages of the life cycle on a separate sheet of paper. Brainstorm a list of products that your team members think will fit within each of the stages. When you have finished, prepare a chart showing your results. As a group, present your chart in class and compare your lists with those developed by other teams. Discuss any of the products on which teams disagree to identify the reasons for the decisions made.

LESSON 3.4
EFFECTIVE SERVICES

GOALS

IDENTIFY important differences between services and products

DESCRIBE how to plan marketing mixes for services

THE EMERGING SERVICE ECONOMY

The number of businesses providing services as their primary activity is growing faster than any other type of business. More than two thirds of all employees in the U.S. now work in service businesses or service jobs. More than half of all purchases made by consumers today are services. The U.S. is changing from the world's leading manufacturing economy into the leading service economy. Companies need to recognize the differences between services and products and how those differences affect marketing decisions.

ON THE $CENE

Jacob was upset with his Internet Service Provider (ISP). He had just been notified that the provider, whose service had been free, was going to start charging $15 per month. Jacob was willing to pay that amount because he had shopped around and saw that other ISPs were charging as much as $30 a month. However, he felt the level of service from his current provider did not meet his expectations if it wasn't free. He often had difficulty connecting, especially in the evening and on weekends. If he was downloading a big file, his connection frequently terminated, requiring him to start the download over. Finally, when he needed technical assistance, the company's help desk staff seemed to know less than he did. Why was Jacob willing to accept a lower level of service before the price increase? What is likely to happen to the ISP based on Jacob's experience?

WHAT ARE SERVICES?

Services are activities of value that do not result in the ownership of anything tangible. Traditional service businesses include movie theaters, insurance companies, banks, car washes, and moving services. However, there are many new types of services such as Internet service providers (ISPs) that connect you to the Internet, personal shoppers, financial planners, and businesses that manage the human resources activities for other businesses.

Services have important characteristics that make them different from products and affect they way they are planned and marketed. Services differ from products in their form, availability, quality, and timing.

Form Services are intangible. They do not include a physical product. They cannot be seen or examined before purchase. They do not exist after they are purchased and used. If you want to go on a Caribbean cruise, you must rely on the descriptions in brochures and videotapes, the advice of a travel agent, or the experiences of friends to select the best cruise. If you get your car washed, you will need to return for the service each time the car needs to be cleaned.

Availability A service cannot be separated from the person or business supplying it. Medical treatment requires a nurse or doctor, a basketball game requires two teams and coaches, and web management services require a webmaster. The availability and the skill of the person providing the service is very important to the customer. You will be quite dissatisfied if the person providing an important service is not able or motivated to complete the job on time. If the person cannot provide the service when you want it, you must go without or find another source. If your cable service does not operate due to an electrical outage, you will not be able to view your favorite television program during the scheduled time.

Quality The quality of the service depends on who provides it as well as on where and when that service is provided. An accountant who is not aware of the latest tax laws may have errors in tax returns that are prepared. A pizza delivery service that takes too long or does not have temperature-controlled delivery bags will bring cold pizza to your door. If you rent an automobile at an airport, you expect it to be clean and in good operating condition. An effective service business needs to be able to control the quality of services and insure that customers get the same quality time after time.

Timing A service cannot be stored or held until the consumer needs it. After a movie starts in a theater, it is no longer available in its complete form until it is replayed. If the tables at a restaurant are filled, no one else can be seated at that time. Likewise, a city bus service runs its buses on a regular schedule even if there are not enough customers to fill the bus at a specific time.

In small groups, identify one service business that primarily serves other businesses and one that primarily serves individual consumers. Develop a chart for each business that describes its target market and marketing mix. Discuss the form, timing, availability, and quality of service offered by each business to its customers.

CHECKPOINT

What are the four ways in which services differ from tangible products?

_____

_____

MARKETING SERVICES

By understanding the unique characteristics of services, managers in charge of planning and marketing services can do a better job of meeting customer needs. Consider the planning that must be done by the manager of a service business such as a fitness center to make sure the business offers the best level of customer service possible for its customers.

THE MARKETING MIX FOR SERVICES

Each of the attributes of a service must be considered when developing the marketing mix. Those attributes can be matched to each of the mix elements—product, distribution, promotion, and price. Each mix element is an important part of marketing services. The company must offer an important service and make sure it is understandable to the customer. It must distribute the service conveniently to the target market. Promotion must effectively communicate the unique qualities of the service in understandable ways. Finally, the price must meet customers' expectations of a good value.

CHANGES IN SERVICE BUSINESSES

Successful service businesses are constantly searching for better ways to provide services. Some of those ways include more careful hiring and training of employees, identifying service quality standards and determining ways to maintain those standards, and using technology to improve the delivery and availability of services. The Internet is providing both opportunities and challenges for service businesses. It is easier to get information to customers using the Internet. Pizzas, CDs, and videotapes can now be ordered online. Consumers can download movies and can even place grocery orders and have products delivered to their door.

Franchising allows a service to be provided in a variety of locations while maintaining a consistent image and level of quality. A person buys a franchise and gets the help and expertise of the parent company in planning and managing the service business. Examples include video rentals, tax preparation and legal services, and home repair and home cleaning franchises.

Managers of service businesses are learning that the marketing orientation is just as meaningful to their companies as it is to businesses that produce and sell products. Extended hours, more locations, customized services, and follow-up activities with customers to ensure satisfaction are all ways that businesses are attempting to meet customer needs.

COMMUNICATE

Service businesses often design a brochure to communicate the intangible features and benefits of their service to customers. Select a service business from your community. Write the copy for a brochure for the business that explains the form, timing, quality, and availability of the service.

CHECKPOINT

Why is communication so important to service businesses?

_____

_____

THINK CRITICALLY

1. Why does the fact that most services are intangible create difficulty in developing a marketing mix?

because they must distribute the service conveniently to the target market

2. Why do service businesses frequently have difficulties providing an adequate supply of the service to meet customer demand?

because the demand usually outways the supply.

3. What are some examples of service businesses that have developed as a result of the growth of the Internet?

Yahoo, monster.com, e-bay,

MAKE CONNECTIONS

4. CAREER PLANNING There are an increasing number of career opportunities in service business for people with varying amounts of education and with different skills and interests. Use career-planning resources in your school's career center, library, or the Internet. Identify at least three service jobs that appeal to you. Locate one job that requires a high school diploma, one that requires a college degree, and one that requires a high level of technical skill. Prepare a short, written description of each job and share the information with other students in your class.

5. RESEARCH Work with a small group of students to complete this activity. A local auto repair business has asked your group to develop a set of five service standards that will help the company meet customer expectations. An example of a standard is "All repairs will be completed at the time promised to the customer or the customer will be notified at least three hours in advance of a delay." To help develop the standards, gather information from several car owners about their experiences with auto repair businesses. Using word-processing software, prepare a one-page document that lists and explains the five service standards.

REVIEW

CHAPTER SUMMARY

LESSON 3.1 The Product
A. The product is the mix element that most businesses consider first when planning a marketing mix. It also is the first consideration for consumers as they determine what they plan to purchase.

B. The product or service as a marketing mix element includes anything offered to the customer by the business that will be used to satisfy needs.

LESSON 3.2 Product Planning
A. Companies can reduce the rate of product failure by improving their understanding of consumer needs and competition.

B. Businesses need a process to identify and develop new products. The process should eliminate products that are not likely to be successful. It should ensure that the products meet an important market need, can be produced at a reasonable price, and will be competitive.

LESSON 3.3 Product Life Cycles
A. Analyzing a product life cycle aids marketers in understanding its competition and developing an effective marketing mix.

B. Successful products move through predictable stages that show how profits and sales change as competition increases.

LESSON 3.4 Effective Services
A. The number of businesses providing services as their primary activity is growing faster than any other type of business.

B. Services differ from products in form, availability, quality, and timing.

VOCABULARY BUILDER

Choose the term that best fits the definition. Write the letter of the answer in the space provided. Some terms may not be used.

____d____ **1.** Anything offered to a market by the business to satisfy needs

____c____ **2.** A name, symbol, word, or design that identifies a product, service, or company

____f____ **3.** Assisting in the design and development of products and services that will meet the needs of prospective customers

____e____ **4.** The stages of sales and profit performance through which all brands of a product progress as a result of competition

____a____ **5.** Activities of value that do not result in the ownership of anything tangible

____b____ **6.** A unique, memorable quality of a brand, such as quality, low price, or innovation

____h____ **7.** Added to improve the basic product

____g____ **8.** Sample developed for expensive or risky products

a. brand
b. feature
c. image
d. product
e. product life cycle
f. product/service planning
g. prototype
h. services

POINT YOUR BROWSER

b2000.swep.com

REVIEW CONCEPTS

9. What are consumers most concerned about when they purchase a product?

Will it last, and was it worth the cost.

10. Why must businesses be careful in planning new products?

They must be careful because they could be a bust.

11. What are the three levels of product planning for businesses?

- Conduct research
- Develop the marketing mix
- Conduct market mix

12. What are the five components of the product mix element?

Basic product   Brand + image
features
Packaging
support sources

13. Why are marketers in a good position to understand customers?

because they deal with them on a daily basis.

14. What are three roles for marketers in the product development process?

Conduct research
develop marketing mix
conduct market tests

15. Describe the steps in the new product planning process.

Idea development   Product development
Idea screening   Product introduction
Strategy development
Financial Analysis

16. How do sales and profits change over the four stages of the product life cycle?

_____

_____

_____

_____

17. How does the amount and type of competition differ between the introduction and maturity stages of the product life cycle?

_____

_____

_____

_____

18. How is the U.S. economy changing in terms of the types of businesses and jobs?

_____

_____

_____

_____

19. What are four ways that services differ from products?

_____

_____

_____

_____

APPLY WHAT YOU LEARNED

20. Provide an example of a basic, enhanced, and extended product.

_____

_____

_____

_____

21. What are some ways that businesses can get ideas for new products from customers without actually talking to the customers?

_____

_____

_____

22. How is a business that has strong brand loyalty from its customers able to compete more effectively in the maturity and decline stages of the product life cycle?

_____

_____

MAKE CONNECTIONS

23. ADVERTISING Select four print advertisements from magazines and newspapers that advertise a service. Choose two ads that have copy and images that you think are effective in helping customers understand what they will receive when they purchase the service. Choose two others that you think are ineffective. Using a computer and word processing software, write a two-page paper that explains why the first two ads were effective and why the other two were ineffective.

24. PROBLEM SOLVING Work with a team of three other students. Select a product that the team agrees is not as effective as it could be. Make a list of the product's problems. Then brainstorm to develop a new product that improves on the problems of the selected product. Create a model or an illustration of the new product to show to other class members. Present your team's model in class, explaining the improvements your team has made and the problems you were solving.

25. BUSINESS MATH A company has determined that one of its products has moved into the maturity stage of the product life cycle and is facing more intense price competition. The company is analyzing several possible price reductions to determine the effect of each on profits. Using the following table and spreadsheet software, calculate the total revenue and the profit or loss for each possible price.

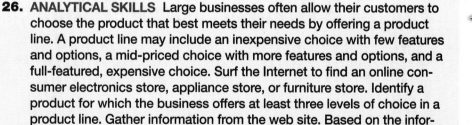

Sale Price	Estimated units sold	Total Revenue	Expenses	Profit or Loss
$20.50	8,530		$180,000	
$19.25	11,860		$230,400	
$18.00	15,620		$275,120	
$16.70	18,240		$301,200	

26. ANALYTICAL SKILLS Large businesses often allow their customers to choose the product that best meets their needs by offering a product line. A product line may include an inexpensive choice with few features and options, a mid-priced choice with more features and options, and a full-featured, expensive choice. Surf the Internet to find an online consumer electronics store, appliance store, or furniture store. Identify a product for which the business offers at least three levels of choice in a product line. Gather information from the web site. Based on the information you gather, prepare a chart that describes the following elements of the marketing mix for each level of the product line: the basic product, features, options, services, brand name, image, price.

CHAPTER 4

DISTRIBUTION AND GLOBAL MARKETING

CAREERS IN MARKETING

UNITED STATES POSTAL SERVICE

The U.S. Postal Service (USPS) operates one of the largest distribution systems in the world. You know the USPS because it delivers your mail. The USPS also competes with FedEx and UPS in the business-to-business package and document-delivery market.

The USPS has been hard hit by the amount of correspondence transmitted electronically. To compete more effectively, it is creating a new business-to-business sales force. Sales positions will be offered to creative and goal-oriented sales professionals wanting to work in a team-selling environment.

Sales Specialists lead an account team of operations, customer relations, and technical support personnel. They develop and present reports, cost/benefit analysis summaries, and comprehensive sales plans for business prospects.

Qualified applicants need extensive business-to-business sales experience, leadership abilities, and an understanding of e-commerce, distribution, and customer service standards.

THINK CRITICALLY

1. Why is the business-to-business market important to the USPS?
2. Why do you think business-to-business sales experience is more important than educational background for this position?

The Chapter 4 video for this module introduces the concepts in this chapter.

PROJECT
Getting Products to Customers

PROJECT OBJECTIVES

■ Identify appropriate channels of distribution for a product and the activities that are part of its distribution

■ Describe the roles of wholesalers and retailers in product distribution

■ List important factors in distributing products to international markets

GETTING STARTED

Read through the Project Process below. Make a list of materials and information you will need. Decide how you will get the needed materials or information.

■ Your class is planning to produce and distribute school mascot key holders to be sold in your school and to other schools. The key holder is a plastic, two-sided button with a customized mascot picture printed on one side and the year of a student's graduation printed on the other side. It has a coiled plastic ring attached to hold keys or other objects.

■ Your team is responsible for planning the distribution mix element for the product.

PROJECT PROCESS

Part 1 LESSON 4.1 The product can be sold through several distribution channels. Identify two target markets for which you can use a direct channel of distribution and two for which an indirect channel of distribution will be used. For one channel of distribution identify the activities that must be completed to make the key holders available to the target market.

Part 2 LESSON 4.2 Use a business directory or other information sources to identify possible wholesalers and retailers who might be a part of your channel of distribution.

Part 3 LESSON 4.3 Describe reasons for and against distributing the product to international customers.

Project Wrap-up As a class, discuss how decisions made about the distribution process for the key holders affect each of the other mix elements, customer satisfaction, and the profits or losses that will result for your class.

LESSON 4.1
DISTRIBUTION CHANNELS

GOALS

DIFFERENTIATE between direct and indirect distribution channels

IDENTIFY the important decisions that must be made in distribution planning

THE DISTRIBUTION FUNCTION

Marketing is a term that became popular in the last half of the 20th century. Businesses recognized the importance of the many marketing functions and activities needed to develop satisfying exchanges with customers. Prior to that time, when companies wanted to improve the exchange process, they concentrated on distribution. While today distribution is just one of many marketing activities, it is very important in ensuring customer satisfaction. If customers cannot locate the product, cannot conveniently obtain it, or receive it late or damaged, they will be very dissatisfied. As one of the four

ON THE $CENE

Consider a movie that has just been released on videotape or DVD. Where are all of the possible places customers would be able to obtain a copy? Of all the possibilities, which would you likely choose? What factors would you consider in making the decision? Movie production companies obtain a large percentage of their revenues from the sale and rental of movies once they are no longer shown in theaters. Usually those sales and rentals determine whether the movie is profitable or not. Compare three different places that you can buy or rent a movie. How are they similar or different in terms of choice of movies, availability of the movies you want to watch, prices, and customer service? What influences your choice of where and how you obtain movies to watch?

marketing mix elements, **distribution** involves determining the best methods and procedures to use so prospective customers can locate, obtain, and use a business's products and services.

REDUCING DISCREPANCIES

The goal of marketing is the successful exchange of products and services between businesses and their customers. No matter how good a product is, a company cannot make a profit unless it fills orders correctly and delivers the product undamaged and on time to the correct locations. Successful exchanges are not easy to carry out.

Several discrepancies exist between producers and consumers. Producers manufacture large quantities of one or a very few products. Consumers want small quantities of a variety of products. Producers manufacture products at a specific time and in a particular location. That time and location do not typically match the place and time consumers need the product. Distribution systems are designed to get the types and quantities of products customers want to the locations where and when they want them.

DIRECT AND INDIRECT DISTRIBUTION

The routes products follow in moving from the producer to the consumer, including all related activities and participating organizations, are called **channels of distribution**. Producers need distribution channels whether they make products for consumers or other businesses. The channels that products follow may be short and simple or long and complex. The shortest path is for the producer to sell directly to the user. The longest path can include a retailer, a wholesaler, and other businesses. When producers sell directly to the consumer, it is called **direct distribution**. When distribution involves other businesses in addition to the producer, it is called **indirect distribution**.

Adding businesses to the channel makes the channel more complex and difficult to control. However, using businesses that have particular expertise in transportation, product handling, or other distribution activities may result in improved distribution or actual cost savings. The activities that need to be performed as a product moves from producer to consumer will help to determine the number and types of businesses in the channel.

Direct Channels Direct distribution, sometimes called *direct marketing*, means the producer sells and distributes its products to consumers. The company is responsible for the equipment, activities, and personnel needed to complete all of the distribution activities. That can include salespeople, warehouses, trucks, order-processing procedures, and customer service. The company may share some of the activities with the consumer. For example, the company might maintain a large warehouse at the production facility. Customers are responsible for transporting their purchases from the warehouse.

Indirect Channels When producers cannot or choose not to perform all marketing activities, they need an indirect channel of distribution. Much time would be wasted if all exchanges of products and services occurred directly between producers and consumers. Think of all of the products and services you purchase in just one week. What if you had to locate and contact each manufacturer, agree on a price, and find a way to get the product from the business to your home? You would spend most of your time just obtaining the things you need to purchase.

COMMUNICATE

You want to open a small store to sell the products of local craftspeople. Prepare a three-minute speech to convince them it will be better for them if you sell their products than for them to sell directly to consumers.

When other businesses enter the channel of distribution, they take over many responsibilities and save you a lot of time. The business determines your needs and the needs of many customers like you. It then contacts the manufacturers of the needed products, purchases what it believes it can sell, and has the products shipped to one location. You can visit the business and purchase many of the products you need in the same shopping trip. In addition to saving you time, the businesses should be effective at locating and purchasing the needed products and finding the most efficient ways to ship them to their locations.

The most common types of businesses involved in indirect channels of distribution are wholesalers and retailers. However, many specialized marketing businesses often are involved including sales and telemarketing businesses, transportation companies, businesses that provide financing and credit, and others.

CHECKPOINT

What is the difference between direct and indirect distribution?

_____

_____

DISTRIBUTION ACTIVITIES

Just as with product/service planning, there are many possible decisions about the locations and methods used to make products available to customers. Some important questions that should be answered in planning distribution include the following.

- Where will the customer want to be able to obtain the product?
- Where will the customer use the product?
- Are there special requirements to transport, store, or display the product?
- When should distribution occur?
- Who should be responsible for each type of distribution activity?

SELEOT A OHANNEL OF DISTRIBUTION

From the available channels of distribution ranging from simple to complex, producers must decide which channel or channels will best fit their needs. Producers generally prefer to use as few channels and channel members as possible. Sometimes producers need to use more than one channel to achieve the widest distribution for their product or to sell to different target markets. The factors businesses consider when deciding which channels to use include distance, perishability, special handling, and number of customers.

Distance If customers are located very close to the producer there is less need for channel members. More channel members will be needed as the distance from producer to consumer increases.

Perishability Highly perishable products require rapid and careful handling. Those products, such as sea food, fresh fruit, and flowers are often marketed directly to the consumer or through a very short channel.

Speoial handling If the product is delicate or easily damaged it requires special handling and shipping procedures or equipment. It is likely to pass through as few channel members as possible. Manufacturers of complex medical equipment, for example, sell directly to hospitals.

Number of oustomers The greater the number of customers, the more channel members there usually will be. If a manufacturer of customized construction equipment sells to a few large contractors, a short channel will be used.

TRANSPORTATION

Businesses must determine how to physically transport the products from the producer to the consumer. Factors to consider in shipping include the size, shape, and weight of the goods. Also, certain goods are fragile and may need special care in handling. Transportation choices will differ for medical supplies needed in a few hours versus building materials needed in several weeks.

Another shipping-related issue is cost. In addition to the basic transportation charges, there are the costs of packaging products for shipment, insurance, and often storing products before, during, and after delivery to the buyer. The most commonly used transportation methods are railroads, trucks, airplanes, and ships. A business may use more than one type of transportation depending on the requirements for the shipment.

PRODUOT HANDLING

Product handling is important in order to avoid delayed, lost, or damaged shipments. Most products are handled several times on their way from producer to consumer. Businesses look for ways to improve packaging, more efficient procedures for packing and unpacking, and better equipment for handling and storing products.

An important part of product handling is keeping track of the products. Businesses and customers want to know where products are in the distribution channel and when they will be delivered. Careful record keeping is essential to route products correctly. Most businesses use bar coding to track products during distribution. For more information on bar coding, see the Tech Talk feature on the next page.

TECH TALK

BAR CODE DATA Bar coding products is a widely used method for tracking products during distribution. Bar codes are product identification labels containing a unique set of vertical bars that scanning equipment can read. Each product or container has a bar code that is read as the product moves through the channel to track its progress. The data gathered is used to prepare reports for management.

THINK CRITICALLY What type of management reports do you think can be created using bar code data?

STORAGE

Consumers typically do not buy products as soon as they are produced. Manufacturers and other channel members must store the products until they are ready for distribution and sale. Buildings such as warehouses and distribution centers are needed to store large quantities of products until they can be sold.

Handling products and storing them for a long time is expensive. Also, moving them around increases the chances for damage. For more efficient handling with less risk of damage, many companies now use mechanical equipment and robots to handle products. Computers control both the equipment and the robots as products are moved into storage and subsequently removed for shipment.

ORDER PROCESSING

Customers place orders in a number of ways. They may visit a retail store or submit an order using a salesperson, mail, telephone, computer, or fax. When an order is received, employees process the order and bill the customer. If customers have questions or problems with the order, employees must handle them in a friendly and courteous fashion. Most companies now have automated order processing using computers and the Internet. That way the manufacturer, channel members, or customers can track the order at any time.

CHECKPOINT

What are the major factors to be considered when a business selects a channel of distribution?

_____

_____

THINK CRITICALLY

1. What discrepancies exist between producers and consumers?

The prices are a discrepancy between the producers + consumers

2. What are some ways a manufacturer can use to insure the effectiveness of an indirect channel of distribution?

They can choose which channel would suit them best

3. Why are the needs and preferences of consumers so important in planning distribution?

They always want to satis

4. What are some ways that computers are used to improve distribution?

MAKE CONNECTIONS

5. CRITICAL THINKING The four primary transportation methods used in product distribution are airplane, truck, railroad, and ship. Create a spreadsheet listing the four methods of transportation as column headings. Then using resources available to you, identify three products under each of the methods that are primarily transported using the method. Review the products you have identified and prepare a one paragraph statement for each method that describes the reasons a company might select that method for transporting its products.

6. DECISION MAKING Magazines are distributed in a number of ways using both direct and indirect channels of distribution. Working as a team with several other students, brainstorm as many places as you can identify where consumers can purchase magazines. Then using a graphics computer software program, diagram two direct and two indirect channels of distribution that a magazine publisher can use to distribute its magazines. Present your diagrams in class, and discuss the advantages and disadvantages of each channel choice. Compare your answers with those of other teams.

LESSON 4.2
WHOLESALERS AND RETAILERS

IDENTIFY benefits of including a wholesaler in a channel of distribution

DISCUSS important marketing activities performed by retailers

WHOLESALERS AS CHANNEL MEMBERS

In order for a product to be sold, all of the marketing functions need to be performed. In a direct channel, the manufacturer and the customer are the only ones who perform the functions. They can be shifted and shared, but they cannot be eliminated. If the producer or consumer is unwilling or unable to perform some of the functions, an indirect channel of distribution is needed. Wholesalers and retailers are the major businesses participating in an indirect channel. They provide the marketing functions that are not completed by producers and consumers.

Common indirect channels of distribution include a manufacturer, a retailer who sells the product of several manufacturers, and the consumers

ON THE $CENE

Outlet malls are becoming increasingly popular. The manufacturers of the products sold usually own the stores in those malls. Consumers are attracted to the stores because they think prices will be significantly lower. However, the same brands of merchandise sold in outlet malls are still purchased by consumers in other stores. In your experience, how does the selection, quality, and age of products sold in outlet malls compare to the same brands sold in other stores? What are reasons people might shop for the brands in other stores, and may be willing to pay higher prices for their purchases?

who purchase from retailers. In situations where channels are long, many products must be sold, or target markets have diverse needs, the traditional channel expands to include a wholesaler.

Wholesalers are companies that assist with distribution activities between businesses. Wholesalers seldom sell products to individual consumers but provide marketing activities as a part of the channel of distribution between producers and retailers.

BENEFITS OF WHOLESALERS

Wholesalers are involved in marketing because they may be able to provide one or more of the needed marketing activities better or at a lower cost than the manufacturer or retailer. For example, a small retailer is not able to purchase most products in the large quantities required by the manufacturer. A wholesaler combines the orders of several small retailers to make the purchase. Shipments to several businesses in the same location are combined to save transportation costs.

A manufacturer usually tries to produce products on a regular basis throughout the year. Consumer demand for the products may be seasonal with most of products purchased during a few months. If the manufacturer does not have the space to store the products until they can be sold, it may use wholesalers who specialize in storage and inventory management.

WHOLESALE ACTIVITIES

Typical wholesaling activities include buying, selling, transporting, and storing products. Wholesalers accumulate the products of many manufacturers, develop assortments for the retail customers they serve, and then distribute the products to them. Some wholesalers provide very specialized activities such as financing the inventories of manufacturers until they can be sold. They also may extend credit to retailers to enable them to purchase.

Wholesalers are important sources of information for other channel members. Many wholesalers offer marketing research and marketing information services. They provide manufacturers and retailers data that will help improve their operations and decisions.

They assist manufacturers in determining needs of retailers and consumers and provide market and product information to retailers. Most wholesalers also promote their products, often in the form of catalogs, salespeople, or Internet sites.

Computer technology can process orders more rapidly and keep track of the quantity and location of products. New methods of storing and handling products reduce product damage, the cost of distribution, and the time needed to get products from the manufacturer to the customer. Wholesalers also provide additional services to their

WORKSHOP

As a class, use a business directory to identify several wholesalers in your area. List the products they sell and the types of customers they serve. Discuss why the wholesalers are needed in the channel of distribution.

customers such as 24-hour ordering and emergency deliveries, and even specialized branding and packaging services so smaller retailers can have their own brand names on products.

CHECKPOINT

What benefits do wholesalers provide to small retailers?

_____

_____

THE ROLE OF RETAILERS

The final business organization in an indirect channel of distribution for consumer products is a **retailer**. Retailers accumulate the products their customers need by buying from manufacturers or wholesalers.

RETAIL ACTIVITIES

Retailers display a variety of products and provide information so customers can evaluate them. Most retailers have salespeople to assist customers with making informed purchase decisions. Retailers provide a variety of services to make it easy for customers to shop and buy including accepting credit cards or providing other credit choices, and offering product delivery, installation, and repair services.

In addition to serving consumers, retailers offer benefits to wholesalers and manufacturers. Besides selling the products of manufacturers, they complete many other marketing functions. They store inventory, assume risk and provide financing. Some retailers even take responsibility for transporting products from the manufacturer to their stores. Retailers have large budgets to promote the products they sell.

TYPES OF RETAILERS

Because there are so many consumers, and because their needs and purchasing behaviors are so different, retail businesses develop to respond to those differences. A way of categorizing retailers is by the types of products offered. Some retailers specialize in one or a few product categories, while others offer customers a wide range of products.

Single- or limited-line stores offer products from one category of merchandise or closely related items. Examples include food, hardware, apparel, lawn and garden, or candle shops.

BUSINESS MATH CONNECTION

Manufacturers offer discounts to channel members for providing various marketing functions. The discounts are often stated as a percentage of the suggested retail price and are expressed as 40/15, for example. The first number 40 is the percentage discount for a retailer. The second number 15 is the percentage discount for a wholesaler. Using the 40/15 discount rate, what price would a retailer and wholesaler pay for a product that retails for $860?

SOLUTION

Selling price − (Selling price × Retailer discount) = Retailer's price
   $860   − ($860   ×   0.40   ) = $516

Retail price − (Retail price × Wholesaler's discount) = Wholesaler's price
   $516   − ($516   ×   0.15   ) = $438.60

Mixed merchandise stores offer products from several different categories. Common examples of mixed merchandise retailers are supermarkets, department stores, and large drug stores all of which sell many categories of products.

Superstores are very large stores that offer consumers wide choices of products. Most superstores are mixed merchandise businesses offering a variety of product categories so consumers can use the business for one-stop shopping. Examples are Sam's Club and Costco. Other superstores sell products in a limited category but offer consumers many choices of brands, products, and features within that category such as Best Buy that sells consumer electronics and appliances, or CarMax that sells used automobiles.

A unique category of retail businesses is non-store retailing. *Non-store retailing* sells directly to the consumer's home rather than requiring the consumer to travel to a store. Two of the most common forms of non-store retailing are door-to-door selling and catalog sales. Other types include vending machines, telephone sales, televised shopping clubs, and direct mail selling. Today, Internet sales have become a popular form of non-store retailing.

CHECKPOINT ✓

List four types of retail businesses.

THINK CRITICALLY

1. Why must all marketing functions be performed by some member of a channel of distribution?

because if they don't the distribution will be unsuccessful.

2. Why would a large retailer want to use a wholesaler?

because they could buy in bulk for a cheeper cost.

3. Why is it possible for an indirect channel of distribution that includes a wholesaler and retailers to be more efficient than a direct channel?

because they dont have to go through the effort of making the products.

4. Why is non-store retailing popular with many consumers?

because it is the most convenient of them all.

MAKE CONNECTIONS

5. **TECHNOLOGY** Arrange a visit to a large supermarket and an interview with a store manager. Ask the store manager to describe the ways technology is used in the store to assist with product storage, pricing, inventory management, and processing customer purchases and payments. Take careful notes during your visit. Write a two-page paper based on the information you gathered.

6. **RESEARCH** Use the Internet to identify two examples of non-store retailers. One should use the Internet to sell its products and another should use a more traditional method of selling (door-to-door, telemarketing, direct mail, and so on). Identify the businesses that are a part of the channel of distribution used by the retailer. List the marketing activities that are performed by each channel member. Prepare a diagram that illustrates your findings.

LESSON 4.3
GLOBAL MARKETING

MARKETING IN INTERNATIONAL BUSINESS

You live in a global economy. To understand this, you need only examine the products you consume each day. Where are they produced and manufactured? What companies were involved in developing, distributing, pricing, and promoting the products? In most cases, it is difficult to identify a product you use that does not have some type of international connection.

In addition to consuming products that have an international connection, many of the jobs available in business depend on the international economy. The United States is the largest producer of goods and services in the world today. However, it is also the largest importer of products produced in other

ON THE $CENE

Fast-food franchises are well known for using the same marketing mix in each city where they have a business. Restaurants look the same in every location and offer the same product choices, prices, and hours of operation. Even the advertisements are the same. However, when the companies open locations in other countries they often have to make dramatic changes in the products, services, prices, and types of promotion used. Why have franchises tried to keep their marketing mix the same from location to location? Why is it sometimes necessary to make major changes in the mix when moving into international markets?

According to Accenture, a global management and technology consulting firm, Chinese will become the most-used language on the Internet by 2007.

countries. Without international trade to provide markets for U.S. products and to obtain products for distribution and sale to U.S. customers, the economy would be much smaller with fewer jobs. Nearly 20 percent of all goods and services produced in the U.S. is sold in other countries. An estimated one in every fifteen U.S. jobs is directly involved in international business.

Thousands of products and trillions of dollars are exchanged between countries involved in international trade. However, only a small percentage of companies worldwide are actually directly involved in international business. About 10 percent of U.S. businesses and a much smaller percentage of businesses worldwide sell products and services in other countries.

Businesses often consider international trade when sales and profits begin to fall in their own countries or when they begin to face competition from businesses from other countries in their current markets. That may be too late to successfully enter international markets. Businesses should consider international markets any time they are studying possible new markets to enter.

EXPORTING AND IMPORTING

The way most businesses first become involved in international business is through exporting and importing. **Exporting** is selling products and services to markets in other countries. **Importing** is purchasing products and services that are produced in other countries. Businesses often use indirect exporting and importing. That means other companies with expertise in international business are a part of the business's channel of distribution. Rather than directly selling products to other customers in other countries, indirect exporting allows the business to use an export company to make the sales. In the same way, with indirect importing, a business will make purchases from an importer rather than purchasing directly from the foreign producer.

Exporters and importers may be full-service or limited-service businesses. A full-service business completes most or all of the marketing functions. The company would purchase the products, provide transportation to another country, and store the products until they are sold. It would have a sales force to contact potential customers and may offer credit or financing. A limited-service business completes one or a very few marketing activities and relies on other companies for other functions. Once an order has been placed, another business is responsible for transporting the products from one country to another.

JOINT VENTURES AND MULTINATIONAL BUSINESSES

Businesses heavily involved in international business often change the way they operate in other countries. Rather than just exporting or importing products, they establish operations in the countries where they have markets.

It may be difficult or very expensive to establish new businesses in several countries. Business owners may not be confident they have the knowledge and experience for successful foreign operations. One way to overcome those problems is by establishing a joint venture. A **joint venture** is an agreement between independent companies to participate in common business activities. A joint venture developed for international business usually involves a company from each of the countries. Two automobile manufacturers may decide to cooperate in producing an automobile that will be sold in both countries.

Each has an understanding of the customers and competition in their own country and has production facilities and dealers already established. Sometimes a manufacturer in one country will develop a joint venture with a retailer in another country to take advantage of the expertise of each.

Companies that operate in many countries and regularly engage in international business are **multinational businesses**. Multinational businesses think and operate globally. Their managers understand how to plan and market products successfully in many countries and are continuously looking for new opportunities throughout the world. Successful multinational businesses have adopted the marketing concept. They recognize that consumers in various countries have different needs and require unique marketing mixes.

CHECKPOINT ✓

What is the difference between exporting and importing?

INTERNATIONAL MARKETING ACTIVITIES

Every time a product or service is sold to a customer, all of the marketing functions need to be performed. This is true in international business as well. However, companies often make a mistake in believing that a marketing mix that was successful in one country will be successful in another country. While all of the marketing functions will need to be performed, they may be quite different when serving customers in another country.

Product/Service Management Products and services need to be designed to meet the unique needs of a target market. Often fewer features and options are offered on products sold in other countries. Packaging may need to be redesigned to offer additional protection for shipping and storage. A brand name may not translate well into another language. There may be quite different expectations for customer service offered with the product.

Distribution Distribution procedures are often a challenge in international marketing. Decisions must be made on how to move the product from one country to another and then distribute it to the locations where it will be sold. Activities must be carefully timed to make sure products are available to customers when they want them. There may be laws that restrict distribution or require that local companies participate in the distribution process.

Selling A country's customs are very important in selling. Salespeople are involve in face-to-face contact with customers. Body language, forms of greetings, being too formal or informal, and customs such as presenting business cards and gifts play an important role in successful selling.

Marketing-Information Management Accurate and adequate market information is essential for planning marketing. Marketing research will be needed to identify target markets and their needs. Research procedures

Identify a product you use or consume that is produced in another country. Describe the marketing mix used to sell the product in the U.S. Discuss with other students ways you think the mix differs from what would be used to sell the product in its home country.

BLURRED BORDERS AND THE LAW

Use of the Internet blurs the geographic borders between countries. However, the laws of a country are applied as if those borders do exist. What happens when something is legal in one country but illegal in another? Napster could not legally continue to allow people to exchange music files in the U.S. But what if it was legal to do so in India? Could the company relocate its headquarters to that country and then continue its service? The European Community has made it illegal for companies to collect and share a variety of personal information about consumers. U.S. companies routinely gather that type of information as part of their marketing research activities. Can U.S. companies be held liable if they collect information from European customers who shop via the Internet? New technology will force countries to reevaluate their laws and how they are enforced.

THINK CRITICALLY Do you think a company should relocate to another country to avoid laws it does not like? Should countries attempt to agree on laws to guide Internet business practices? Why or why not?

that are useful in one country may not be acceptable in another. Companies need to pay particular attention to cultural and social differences, economic conditions, legal and political structures, and differences in technology.

Financing If an exporter or importer will sell a product, the company may need to extend credit or provide financing for that company until the products are sold. Banks specializing in international finance are available to help with financial planning and management.

Pricing Prices to be charged must be calculated carefully to cover the costs of international business activities. The prices have to be acceptable to customers and competitive with the products of competitors in each market. The form of payment, value of currency, and consumer credit practices might be quite different.

Promotion Communicating information to prospective customers through advertising and other promotional methods is essential if a product is going to be successfully sold in another country. Effective communication relies on the careful choice of language and images that are understood by the target market. Often images and words don't translate well into another language and culture.

Name the seven marketing functions to be performed in conducting international business.

_____

_____

THINK CRITICALLY

1. Why do many companies fail to consider international marketing when selecting target markets?

_____

_____

_____

2. What are the possible disadvantages of participating in a joint venture with a business from another country?

_____

_____

_____

3. Why is managing marketing information such an important function when marketing in another country?

_____

_____

_____

MAKE CONNECTIONS

4. FINANCE Countries have different forms of currency and the value of each currency changes in relation to that of other countries based on economic conditions. Use the Internet to gather the information about the name of the primary currency for each country listed in the following table and the current exchange rate for that currency in relationship to the U.S. dollar. Use spreadsheet software to calculate the cost of a product that costs $85 in the U.S. in each country's currency based on that exchange rate.

Country	Primary Currency	Current value compared to the U.S. dollar	Product Price in Country's Currency
Argentina			
Australia			
Japan			
Italy			
Vietnam			

5. FOREIGN LANGUAGE Select three popular products that have well-known slogans or jingles. If you can speak and write a language other than English, attempt to translate the slogans and jingles into that language. If not, ask for the help of another person who is bilingual or research to find the translations. Identify the words or phrases that do not translate well or that may lead to another meaning than what was intended in the original message. Present your translations in class. Discuss your examples with other students and how the results would affect communications in another country.

REVIEW

CHAPTER SUMMARY

LESSON 4.1 Distribution Channels
A. Distribution is very important in ensuring customer satisfaction. If customers cannot locate the product, cannot conveniently obtain it, or receive it late or damaged, they will be very dissatisfied.

B. Producers must decide which distribution channel or channels will best fit their needs.

LESSON 4.2 Wholesalers and Retailers
A. Wholesalers and retailers are the major businesses participating in an indirect channel.

B. Wholesalers provide marketing activities as a part of the channel of distribution between producers and retailers. Retailers accumulate the products their customers need by buying from manufacturers or wholesalers.

LESSON 4.3 Global Marketing
A. The U.S. is the largest producer of goods and services in the world and the largest importer of products produced in other countries.

B. Marketing mixes may differ widely among countries.

VOCABULARY BUILDER

Choose the term that best fits the definition. Write the letter of the answer in the space provided. Some terms may not be used.

_C_ **1.** Determining the best methods and procedures to use so prospective customers can locate, obtain, and use a business's products and services

_A_ **2.** The routes products follow while moving from the producer to the consumer

_B_ **3.** Producers sell directly to the consumer

_F_ **4.** Distribution involves businesses in addition to the producer

_J_ **5.** Companies that assist with distribution activities between businesses

_I_ **6.** The final business organization in an indirect channel of distribution for consumer products

_D_ **7.** Selling products and services to markets in other countries

_E_ **8.** Purchasing products and services that are produced in other countries

_G_ **9.** An agreement between independent companies to participate in common business activities

a. channels of distribution

b. direct distribution

c. distribution

d. exporting

e. importing

f. indirect distribution

g. joint venture

h. multinational business

i. retailer

j. wholesalers

POINT YOUR
BROWSER

b2000.swep.com

REVIEW CONCEPTS

10. What discrepancies between producers and consumers are reduced with effective distribution?

Some discrepancies would be the time it takes to get the products

11. What two common types of business are involved in indirect distribution but not direct distribution?

2 types of businesses are markets and hardware stores.

12. In what ways can wholesalers benefit manufacturers and retailers?

They can buy in bulk for a cheaper cost.

13. What is a non-store retailer?

A non-store retailer is an online store.

14. Approximately what percent of U.S. businesses buy and sell products in other countries?

about one half of the businesses buy + sell

15. What are the challenges involved in distributing products internationally?

You have to deal with the foreign currency

REVIEW

APPLY WHAT YOU LEARNED

16. Why do many Internet businesses use indirect channels of distribution even though they have direct contact with customers?

because it is easier on the businesses and saves them money

17. What are some examples of products where perishability and special handling are important distribution concerns?

food and fragile furnature are good examples

18. How can having a wholesaler as a part of a channel of distribution benefit consumers?

They can buy in bulk for cheeper price.

19. What advantages and disadvantages do superstores provide for consumers?

They provide large varieties of products but they are of less quality.

20. What characteristics should a company look for when selecting an exporter to help develop international business?

They should check their background and see if they are reliable.

21. Provide examples of how technology can affect each of the marketing mix elements for a company involved in international marketing.

_____

_____

_____

_____

_____

_____

MAKE CONNECTIONS

22. SOCIOLOGY Select a country that interests you as a location for international marketing. Gather information on the country's culture and customs that should be considered when developing a marketing mix. Use a word-processing program to prepare a one-page report on your findings.

23. INTERNATIONAL BUSINESS Use the Internet or a business directory to identify two companies fitting each of the following categories: importer, exporter, joint venture participant, and multinational company. Identify the company's name, address, the products or services it provides, and an Internet address if available.

_____

_____

_____

_____

24. BUSINESS MANAGEMENT Using the Yellow Pages of your community's telephone directory, identify at least ten retailers. Classify the retailers as to whether they are single-line stores, limited-line stores, mixed merchandise stores, superstores, or non-store retailers. Present your findings in a spreadsheet format.

_____

_____

_____

25. RESEARCH Work with a team of other students to complete this activity. Interview a number of people and ask them to identify a negative experience they had when purchasing a product. Record their answers in a notebook. When the interviews are completed, the team should review all of the answers and identify whether the reason related to a distribution activity or some other business activity. Prepare an oral presentation for your class that recommends how companies can improve customer satisfaction using distribution activities.

CHAPTER 5

CAREERS IN MARKETING

ECHOSTAR

For millions of viewers worldwide, an alternative to cable television is satellite TV. EchoStar, headquartered in Littleton, Colorado, is the parent company of DISH Network, a Direct Broadcast Satellite (DBS) system. EchoStar provides equipment and programming to customers. EchoStar customers receive more than 500 television, movie, music, and data channels as well as an Internet connection using an 18-inch receiving disk mounted on their home.

A DISH Network Retention Manager develops plans to retain customers. The Manager tracks retention rates, completes ROI and breakeven analyses, analyzes retention patterns, and studies seasonal trends. The manager also plans research projects to identify ways to increase retention.

The Manager needs a bachelor's degree and three to seven years of marketing experience. Superb analytical skills using Excel and Access as well as excellent written and oral communications are required. The person must be an effective project manager who works well under pressure.

THINK CRITICALLY

1. Why would a business with more than six million customers be concerned about customer retention?
2. Why is the ability to work under pressure important for this position?

PRICE SETTING

LESSONS

5.1 PRICING METHODS

5.2 CREDIT

5.3 ADDED VALUE FOR CUSTOMERS

The Chapter 5 video for this module introduces the concepts in this chapter.

PROJECT
Establish Price and Value

PROJECT OBJECTIVES

■ Identify the various ways that businesses present prices to customers
■ Determine the importance of credit in customer purchasing decisions
■ Describe how customers determine a fair price for products they purchase

GETTING STARTED

Read through the Project Process below. Make a list of materials and information you will need. Decide how you will get the needed materials or information.

■ Identify three products that you will study for this project. One product should sell for less than $5, the second for $50 to $1,000, and the third for more than $1,000.

PROJECT PROCESS

Part 1 LESSON 5.1 For each of the products you have selected, visit businesses, review product catalogs, or use the Internet to find two different prices for each. Create a table that lists the product, the two prices, and the method used to communicate each price to customers. For each of the products, do you think the price listed by the company is the price the customer has to pay? Why or why not?

Part 2 LESSON 5.2 For the most expensive product you chose for the project, identify three businesses that sell the product. Identify and briefly describe the types of credit, if any, each business offers to customers who want to purchase the product. What are the best and worst credit terms available from the three businesses? Do any of the businesses offer a lower price if the customer does not use credit?

Part 3 LESSON 5.3 Rank the three products in terms of the importance of price to the customer when deciding to purchase the product or not. Assign a 1 to the product for which price is the most important factor, 2 for the next most important, and 3 for the least important. Justify your rankings.

Project Wrap-up As a class, discuss how a product's price as well as the availability of credit influences customers' purchase decisions. Compare the importance of price with each of the other mix elements in increasing customer satisfaction.

LESSON 5.1
PRICING METHODS

DISCUSS the importance of pricing in marketing

IDENTIFY how product prices are set

THE IMPORTANCE OF PRICE

How do you decide what you will pay for a product or service? Sometimes you think a price is too high, so you decide not to buy or to look for a lower price from another company. Other times you go ahead and buy even though you would have preferred a lower price.

Customers want value for the money they pay for products and services. On the other hand, businesses need to make a profit on the products and services they sell. You probably don't think about the profit a company will make when you evaluate the price of a product. Companies that think only of profit without considering how customers will view the price of their product will probably end up with many dissatisfied customers.

ON THE $CENE

Everything on sale! Lowest prices of the season! We will not be undersold! You are probably used to these messages blaring from television or radio and jumping out of advertisements in your local newspaper. Many retail businesses plaster their windows and walls with signs advertising low prices, discounts, rebates, and sale prices. How are average consumers affected when they see those signs everywhere and everyday? Are there products that you will not buy unless they are on sale? Are there stores where you know when they advertise a sale that prices will be much lower than regular prices? Identify ways businesses mislead customers with sale prices. What effect do those practices have on you when deciding where to shop?

PRICE IN THE MARKETING MIX

One of the four elements of the marketing mix, **price** is the cost of the product or service paid by the customer. As one of the seven functions of marketing, **pricing** is defined as establishing and communicating the value of products and services to prospective customers. When planning any marketing activity, businesspeople must consider the impact of the cost to the business, the price customers must pay, and the value that is added to the product or service as a result of the activity.

Businesses must plan prices carefully. Prices can be changed much more quickly than other marketing mix elements. Once a product is designed and produced, it is very difficult to change its form or features. Moving a product through a channel of distribution involves many activities and often several companies. The locations where customers can purchase the product are not easy to change either. Finally, with promotion, advertisements must be prepared, media purchased well in advance, and salespeople given product information and training. Changing a price is often as simple as adding a new price sticker or marking out an old price. Even manufacturers can change the price charged by a retailer by offering a coupon or a rebate to customers. Because prices can be changed more rapidly, some businesses are quick to lower a price if they think it will help sell a product. That quick decision may cause the business to lose money.

PRICE AS AN ECONOMIC CONCEPT

An effective price is based on the economic concept of supply and demand. If there is a small quantity of a product or service but a very large demand, the price will usually be quite high. If there is a very large supply of a product or if demand is low, the price will be low. However, price is affected by more than just the quantity of a product available. Customers determine the value they will receive from a product or service. They are willing to pay more for greater value. The value of a purchase results from many factors. Customers think a product is a better value if it is easy to use, more accessible or convenient, or has a desired image.

Prices charged for products and services are important to the businesses selling them as well as to consumers. The price determines how much money a business will have available to cover the costs of designing, producing, and marketing the product. If the price is not high enough to pay those costs and provide a profit, the business will be unable to continue to offer that product. Effective marketing results in satisfaction for both the consumer and the business. A satisfactory price means that the consumer views the purchase as a value. It also means that the business makes a profit on the sale.

What does a satisfactory price mean to customers and to a business?

_____

_____

Work with other class members to identify businesses in your community that you think price products to increase profit, to maximize sales, to meet competition, and to maintain a specific image. Discuss the effect of those pricing decisions on the types of products each business sells and the customers they attract.

DETERMINE PRICES

Determining the best prices to charge for products is not easy. Companies want prices that cover their costs and contribute a reasonable profit. However, consumers don't care about the company's costs or whether the company makes a profit on the sale. They want to get the best value and expect the product to be comparably priced to other similar products.

It is not easy to determine the actual costs for marketing a product or what customers are willing to pay. Many companies do not have enough information to set prices properly. They may base their prices solely on what competitors are charging. They may set their prices high, thinking that they can reduce them if customers are unwilling to pay the original prices. Such practices are risky and may result in unsold products or loss of profits. Prices should be planned as carefully as the other mix elements.

SET PRICING OBJECTIVES

The first step a company takes in planning prices is to determine what objectives it wants to accomplish with the product's price. Examples of possible objectives are to maximize profits, increase sales, meet competition, or maintain an image.

Maximize Profits Companies that seek to maximize profits carefully study consumer demand and determine what customers in the target market are willing to pay for their products. They set prices as high as possible while still satisfying customers. In this way, there is more money to cover the costs of production and marketing and return a profit.

Increase Sales Some companies want prices that achieve the highest possible sales volume. Prices usually will be quite low to encourage customers to buy. Companies using a sales-based objective need to set the price high enough to cover costs. Also, they must have an adequate supply of the products to meet customer demand.

COMPARE ONLINE PRICES The Internet has changed the importance of price for consumers. Prior to the Internet, comparisons usually could be made only among a few local businesses. The customer would have to travel to each business or obtain the catalogs or price lists of other companies. Today, price comparisons are as simple as completing an online search. Within minutes, a consumer can check the price of a product from many businesses. Web sites have been developed that continually gather price information for products and list them for consumers. They can even determine if the product is in stock and how long it will take for the product to be delivered. Because of the Internet, companies now face intense price competition with more competitors than ever before.

THINK CRITICALLY What advantages and disadvantages does a business face when customers can compare prices using the Internet? How can a business compete if it doesn't have the lowest-priced products?

Meet Competition Customers see very few differences in some products. In those instances, it would not be wise for one competitor to charge a higher price than other companies. Customers would be unwilling to pay the higher price. Therefore a business must set its prices in line with those of competitors. In some industries, if one company lowers its prices too much, it will set off a price war and all the companies may end up losing money. This type of competition exists in the airline industry. Thus airlines generally keep the prices of flights to the same cities very similar.

Maintain an Image Companies can use the prices of products to create an image for the product or the company. Many consumers think that price and quality are related. Higher prices generally mean better quality, while lower prices suggest poorer quality. Companies that are building a quality image should maintain higher prices than competitors. Companies appealing to cost-conscious customers need to keep their prices lower than competitors.

CHECKPOINT

Name four possible objectives for planning prices.

_____

_____

SET THE PRICE OF A PRODUCT

The price consumers are charged for a product or service is known as the **selling price**. The price at which a product is sold will determine whether the business is able to make a profit or not. Setting the correct price for a product is one of the most difficult marketing decisions.

DETERMINE SELLING PRICE

The selling price is made up of cost and markup. The largest part of the selling price for most products is the *cost* of the product. For manufacturers this is the cost of producing the product. For wholesalers and retailers it is the cost of purchasing the product. The difference between the cost of the product and the selling price is known as the markup. The **markup** is the amount added to the cost of the goods to cover all other expenses plus a profit.

Selling price = Cost + Markup

Businesses determine the correct percentage, or *rate of markup*, needed to cover expenses and provide a profit. Markups often are calculated as a percentage of the product cost. If the cost of the product to the store is $280 and the rate of markup is 45 percent, the markup will be

Markup = Cost × Rate of markup
Markup = $280 × 0.45
Markup = $126

The selling price will be

Selling price = Cost + Markup
Selling price = $280 + $126
Selling price = $406

A few businesses use a standard markup for the products they sell. All products are originally marked up the same percentage, such as 50 percent, to determine the selling price. Other businesses determine the costs related to specific products or product categories. Then they develop a separate markup percentage for each.

SET EFFECTIVE PRICES

Just because a markup percentage is used to calculate the selling price doesn't mean that is the price customers will pay. You will often see that businesses have to reduce a product's price because an incorrect markup was used. This reduction in price is referred to as a *markdown*.

High markups do not always mean that the business will make a larger profit on the product. Usually a high markup reduces the quantity sold or results in slower sales and higher costs to the business. On the other hand, businesspeople must be careful in using very low markups. While the lower price may result in higher sales, the markup may not cover all expenses.

In some cases, expenses increase because of the costs of handling a larger quantity of products. Marketers must carefully study the effects of different markup percentages before determining the one to be used.

CHECKPOINT

What are the formulas for computing selling price and markup based on cost?

_____

_____

THINK CRITICALLY

1. What are some examples of products you purchase where the price is particularly affected by supply and demand?

_____

_____

_____

2. Why is setting the correct price on a product such a difficult decision?

_____

_____

_____

3. Why would a company want to avoid taking markdowns on a product's price when many consumers are attracted to a business by sale prices?

_____

_____

_____

MAKE CONNECTIONS

4. PSYCHOLOGY Research has shown that the way the price of a product is presented has a psychological effect on consumers. For example, gasoline is often priced with $0.0099 added to the price. If you see gas priced at $1.5999, you will think the price is $1.59 a gallon rather than $1.60. If you see a CD priced at $19.95 you will think the price is $19 rather than $20. Study product prices in stores and in advertisements including sale prices. Find examples that you think have a psychological effect on consumers. Use word-processing software to develop a report that presents the examples and explains how you think the price is designed to affect consumers.

5. BUSINESS MATH Use spreadsheet software to calculate the missing values in the table. The formulas are

Selling price = Cost + Markup

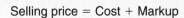

Markup = Cost × Rate of markup

Selling Price	Cost	Markup	Rate of Markup
$1.50	$0.40		
	$44	$22	
		$30	25%
	$6.50	$2.25	
		$534	45%

LESSON 5.2
CREDIT

DESCRIBE factors to consider in offering credit to customers

IDENTIFY important credit and collection procedures used by businesses

THE IMPORTANCE OF CREDIT

What is your perception of the following two statements by an automobile salesperson?

"The retail price of the new Frienza is $26,800."
"You can drive home the new Frienza for $320 per month."

Paying the full price for a new automobile is not possible for most customers. If the auto dealership can assist customers with financing, the monthly payments are affordable. Without credit, many products and services would remain unsold. Developing effective credit policies and procedures is an important marketing activity.

ON THE $CENE

How much credit can you afford? It seems as if every retail store wants you to sign up for its credit card. Offers from MasterCard, Visa, and Discover arrive in your mailbox every day. While credit cards may be easy to obtain, the cost of credit is very high for consumers and businesses alike. Unpaid credit bills quickly add interest so the customer ends up paying a very high price for the products purchased. If credit debts are uncollected by businesses, they will need to add those costs to product prices so customers end up paying higher prices. What advice would you give to a friend who is considering whether to apply for a credit card? Do you think businesses should make credit easy for all of their customers to obtain?

FINANCING BUSINESS SALES AND PURCHASES

In order to satisfy customer needs, a product must be affordable. If products remain unsold because customers cannot afford to purchase them, a business cannot make a profit. By simply reducing the product's price, the company may sell the product—but at a loss. Credit provides a means to meet customer needs at a profit.

Credit is a part of the financing function of marketing. **Financing** includes budgeting for marketing activities, obtaining the necessary financing, and providing financial assistance to customers to assist them with purchasing the organization's products and services. Credit is a very important marketing activity for most businesses. Seldom are all sales made with cash. Credit is provided to customers to help them finance purchases from the business. The business also uses credit to help it finance the purchases of products and services needed to operate the company.

TYPES OF CREDIT

Consumer credit is credit extended by a retail business to a consumer. The credit may be provided by the seller or may be offered by another business that is participating in the marketing process, such as a bank, finance company, or a credit card company like MasterCard or Discover.

Most sales between businesses are made on credit. **Trade credit** is financing offered by one business to another business. This happens because of the time lag between when a sale is negotiated and when the products are actually delivered to the business and then resold to the business' customers. Credit sales are a traditional business practice in many channels of distribution. Businesses expect to be able to wait 30 to 60 days or longer before making payment for their purchases.

Many purchases of companies are very expensive. A computer system, major pieces of equipment, or a new building may cost hundreds of thousands of dollars or more. To be able to afford the purchase, the company will need to obtain financing from a bank or the product's supplier.

CHECKPOINT ✓

What are the two types of credit used in business?

_____

_____

WORKSHOP

Gather information from several companies and financial institutions on the interest rates they charge for credit cards, financing purchases, and personal loans. Make a list of the types of credit and the interest rates listed. Discuss why businesses offer different interest rates and how the interest rates might influence consumer purchase decisions.

DEVELOP CREDIT PROCEDURES

Credit provides a method for obtaining additional customers and sales that otherwise might not be possible with cash sales only. If credit is poorly managed, though, costs may be very high and the money from the sale of products may never be collected from some customers. Businesspeople responsible for credit sales must plan procedures carefully to be sure that credit is a successful part of a marketing strategy. The procedures include developing credit policies, approving credit customers, and developing effective collection procedures.

CREDIT POLICIES

A business must first decide whether or not to offer credit and whether to offer it on all products and for every customer. Next, it must develop a credit plan. The business decides whether it will offer its own credit plan or rely on other companies to offer credit. Finally, the credit terms are developed. The terms include the amount of credit that will be extended, the rate of interest to be charged, and the length of time given to customers before payment is required.

CREDIT APPROVAL

Not all customers are good candidates for credit. If a customer is unable to pay for purchases, the business will lose all of the money invested in producing and marketing the product as well as the cost of extending credit.

A business offering credit needs to determine the characteristics and qualifications of the customers that will be able to pay for credit purchases. Those factors typically include the person's credit history, the resources they have that demonstrate their financial ability, and the sources and amount of money that will be available to make the credit payments.

Most businesses have a credit application procedure in which the applicant provides the needed information. Credit applicants may be asked to provide financial references. These references include banks and other businesses from which they have obtained credit in the past. Businesses use credit services such as Dun & Bradstreet to confirm the information provided by the applicant and to get a report on the creditworthiness of the customer.

BUSINESS MATH CONNECTION

The interest paid on a purchase must be added to the price of the product to determine the total cost to the customer. The interest rate and the length of time the purchase is financed determine the cost of the credit. What is the cost of credit for a product costing $1,200, financed at an interest rate of 12.5%, for 1 year? What is the total cost to the purchaser?

SOLUTION

Product price × Interest rate × Number of years = Interest
$1,200 × 0.125 × 1 = $150

Product price + Interest = Total cost of product
$1,200 + $150 = $1,350

COLLECTIONS

Effective collection procedures are an important part of a credit plan. The procedures are needed so that customers are billed at the appropriate time and pay their accounts when they are due. Because some customers are unable or unwilling to pay their accounts, procedures for collecting overdue accounts are an important part of a credit system.

Most businesses have a percentage of their credit accounts that are never collected. A company can sell its uncollected accounts to

companies that then attempt to make collections. However, the amount received by the business for the sale of the uncollected accounts is usually a small percentage of the actual amount of the original sales.

CHECKPOINT

What happens to a business if credit is poorly managed?

_____

_____

THINK CRITICALLY

1. Why might consumers want to use credit even if they can afford to pay the full price of a product in cash at the time of purchase?

2. Why is the use of credit considered to be a part of marketing planning rather than just a financial activity of a business?

3. Why is it important for businesses to be able to obtain credit for the products they buy that will be resold to their customers?

4. Why do businesses need to gather financial information from a customer before offering credit if the customer already has a credit card?

MAKE CONNECTIONS

5. **BUSINESS LAW** Several federal laws guide businesses in developing credit policies, providing information about credit terms to consumers, and collecting past due accounts. Use the Internet to identify and research one law related to consumer credit. Use a word-processing program to prepare a one-page report on the law. Describe how the law is designed to protect the consumer from unfair credit practices.

6. **TECHNOLOGY** Find a loan calculator on the Internet that will allow you to enter a loan amount, an interest rate, and the number of months or years the money will be borrowed. Use the loan calculator to determine the monthly payment and the total amount of interest paid for the following loans.

   A. Home loan for $185,000 for 30 years at 8.5%

   B. Car loan for $12,800 for 4 years at 12%

   C. Calculate the monthly payments and total interest paid if the interest rate is 3% higher on each loan

   D. Calculate the monthly payments and total interest paid if the interest rate is 2% lower on each loan

   E. If the loan calculator allows, print out a schedule of payments on one of the loans that shows the principal and interest paid each month. Compare how the amounts change over the life of the loan.

LESSON 5.3
ADDED VALUE FOR CUSTOMERS

GOALS

DISCUSS the difference between price and non-price competition

DESCRIBE ways to add customer value with marketing mix elements

REDUCE COMPETITION

Why would someone pay much more for a particular brand of basketball shoes or a designer label of clothing? They could have the same quality at a lower price by choosing a lesser-known brand. Have you ever visited a restaurant where the prices were not listed on the menu? Why would people be willing to order a meal without knowing the amount they will pay?

   Price is one element of a marketing mix. It is the most important element when people will only purchase the product choice that costs the least. At other times, price is almost unimportant. People are willing to pay much more than they have to for quality, image, convenience, or a high level of customer service.

ON THE $CENE

Jacob Foster owns a small supermarket in an upscale neighborhood. A large national wholesale club is being built less than a mile from the location of his store. The wholesale club will sell a number of the same food products that Jacob offers in his store. It also will offer a large number of non-food products that Jacob doesn't offer. He knows that with the purchasing power of a large national company, the wholesale club will be able to sell its products at a lower price than he can. What advice would you give to Mr. Foster about how he might be able to continue to operate profitably when the new store opens?

WORKSHOP

Identify three products that you think represent price competition and three that represent non-price competition. Construct a table that describes each of the marketing mix elements for each of the products. Using the table, discuss with classmates why you think the type of competition exists for each of the products.

PRICE AND NON-PRICE COMPETITION

The type of competition businesses face ranges from very intense to limited. With intense competition, the business has other companies who sell the same products and offer similar marketing mixes. Customers see few if any differences among the products of the competing businesses. They will likely purchase the products from the company that offers the lowest prices. Rivalry among businesses where the primary difference is the price offered is known as **price competition**. Unless a company is very large and efficient, it is difficult to compete on the basis of price alone and still make a profit.

Non-price competition emphasizes factors other than price as the important reason for customers to buy. Customers may see differences among products and companies in terms of their need satisfaction. When differences in product quality, availability, and customer service matter, it may be worth it to customers to pay extra for the added benefits. They will be more careful in comparing the products and services they purchase rather than just selecting the ones with the lowest price.

AVOID PRICE COMPETITION

Would you choose a dentist to complete important dental work just because he or she charged the lowest price for the service? Do you select the cheapest ticket price to attend the concert of your favorite music group? Will you select the least expensive college to attend after high school if it doesn't offer the courses or environment you prefer? Consumers usually are very careful about selecting the products and services that they think will provide the greatest benefit for the money they spend. Businesses that carefully study the needs of their target markets and provide a marketing mix that meets those needs will usually be able to avoid price competition.

CHECKPOINT

What is the difference between price and non-price competition?

_____

_____

_____

ADD VALUE WITH THE MARKETING MIX

Customers consider many factors when making a purchase. They want a product that offers the features and functions they need. They want to be able to obtain the product at a location that is convenient, that they trust, and that offers the customer services they desire. Customers expect to obtain the information and sales help they need to make the most informed decision. They may want to be able to obtain financing from the seller or to be able to pay with a check, debit card, or credit card.

The purchase decision usually comes down to more than the lowest price. Companies need to study all the elements of the marketing mix and compare them to the specific needs of a target market to determine ways to add value for the customer.

Product The customer's perception of value can be changed by making additions to the basic product. New features make the product easier to use or allow it to meet additional customer needs. Packaging changes result in easier handling or storage, less product damage, or a more visible and attractive product. Services, guarantees, and warranties provide greater customer satisfaction and assurance that the company stands behind its products. Products that are clearly designed for a unique market segment will have greater value than those that appear to have been developed for another segment.

Distribution Consumers frequently purchase products that are easily available, attractively displayed, or sold through their favorite stores. If a product is out of stock, the customer is likely to choose another brand. If the product or package has been damaged during shipment, it will remain unsold. Effective customer service including efficient and accurate order processing will often convince a customer to buy the business's products.

Price One of the important ways to add value to the price of a product is by offering credit or other forms of financing. Another way of adding value is to provide complementary products or a larger quantity for a reduced unit price, such as "buy two and get a third item free."

Promotion Communication is an important tool for changing consumer perception of value. An effective advertisement, display, or sales demonstration can provide customers with information on how a product will meet their needs better than other choices. Other types of promotion are used to enhance the value of a product. Some businesses offer prizes and premiums for purchases or use incentives for regular purchasing. Coupons can be used to encourage people to visit a business or purchase a product.

Create an advertisement for a product that emphasizes reasons other than price for consumers to choose that brand. Show the ad to other students in your class and describe how you attempted to create "value" in the advertisement.

THE EXPLODING HISPANIC MARKET

Liz Claiborne Fragrances introduced Mambo, a Latino scent. One of the "got milk" advertisements features an Hispanic man and his young daughter shopping for the ingredients to make a "tres leches," a popular dessert among Latin families. McDonald's features Cuban sandwiches and "dulce de leche McFlurry" in South Florida restaurants. The interest in Hispanic markets grew rapidly as the number of Hispanic Americans in the U.S. population increased to 33 million in the 2000 census. Representing more than 12% of the national population, it is the fastest-growing minority segment. Immigrants who bring the Spanish language and their Latin culture with them to their new homes account for much of this growth. Businesses are moving at full speed to meet the needs of this important consumer group. Among the top advertisers in the Hispanic market are Procter and Gamble, MCI/WorldCom, AT&T, Sears, and McDonald's. The top ten U.S. Hispanic markets had a total of $199 billion in purchasing power in 2000.

THINK CRITICALLY What advantages do companies have when they produce unique products and develop specific advertisements for the Hispanic market? Why did it take the 2000 census information to cause many businesses to begin to recognize the Hispanic market?

CHECKPOINT

Name one way each of the mix elements can be used to enhance the value of a product.

_____

_____

THINK CRITICALLY

1. What causes price to be the most important mix element for some customers?

_____

_____

_____

2. What are the characteristics of companies who are successful using price competition?

_____

_____

_____

3. Why will the price of a product likely be higher if a business is trying to increase profits rather than trying to increase sales?

_____

_____

_____

4. What are some ways that contests, games, and other similar promotional activities can be misused by businesses?

_____

_____

_____

MAKE CONNECTIONS

5. TECHNOLOGY Work in small groups to complete this exercise. List each of the marketing mix elements on the board. Each student in turn should go to the board and list an example of how technology and the Internet have added value to products and services. The item should be listed under the appropriate mix element. Continue until all possible examples have been listed. Discuss the items to determine if everyone agrees on the placement of the items under the mix elements. Which of the mix elements seems to have been affected most by technology?

6. DEBATE Form two teams to debate the following issue:

"Consumers benefit when businesses engage in price competition rather than non-price competition."

Use the following space to take notes of the arguments for or against the issue presented during the debate. After the debate has been completed, write a 100-word statement in support or opposition to the issue. After the statements have been prepared, poll all students to see the number who agree with the statement and the number who disagree with it.

_____

_____

_____

_____

REVIEW

CHAPTER SUMMARY

LESSON 5.1 Pricing Methods

A. Customers want value for the money they pay for products and services. Companies that think only of profit without considering price and value will probably have many dissatisfied customers.

B. Prices must be planned carefully by businesses. Changing a price is as simple as changing the price tag or adding a sale price.

LESSON 5.2 Credit

A. Credit is provided to customers to help them finance purchases from the business. The business also uses credit to help it finance the purchases of products and services needed to operate the company.

B. A company offering credit needs to develop credit policies and a credit plan. The business must decide whether it will offer its own credit plan or rely on other companies to offer credit.

LESSON 5.3 Added Value for Customers

A. Sometimes price is the most important marketing mix element. At other times, price is almost unimportant. People are willing to pay more for quality, image, convenience, or superior customer service.

B. Companies need to study each element of the marketing mix and compare them to the specific needs of a target market to determine ways to add value for the customer.

VOCABULARY BUILDER

Choose the term that best fits the definition. Write the letter of the answer in the space provided. Some terms may not be used.

_____ **1.** The actual cost of a product or service paid by the customer

_____ **2.** Establishing and communicating the value of products and services to prospective customers

_____ **3.** The price consumers are charged for a product or service

_____ **4.** An amount added to the cost of a product to determine the selling price

_____ **5.** Budgeting for marketing activities, obtaining the necessary financing, and providing financial assistance to customers to assist them with purchasing the organization's products and services

_____ **6.** Credit extended by a retail business to the final consumer

_____ **7.** Financing offered by one business to another business

_____ **8.** Rivalry among businesses where the primary difference is the price offered

_____ **9.** Emphasizes factors other than price as the important reason for customers to buy

a. consumer credit

b. financing

c. markup

d. non-price competition

e. price

f. price competition

g. pricing

h. selling price

i. trade credit

REVIEW CONCEPTS

POINT YOUR BROWSER

b2000.swep.com

10. What is the difference between the customer's view of price and a business's view of price?

_____

_____

_____

_____

11. How does the economic concept of supply and demand affect the price of a product?

_____

_____

_____

_____

12. How does providing credit make a product more affordable for consumers?

_____

_____

_____

_____

13. How does the financing function of marketing relate to the concept of credit?

_____

_____

_____

_____

14. Under what circumstances might a consumer pay more than the lowest possible price for a product?

_____

_____

_____

_____

15. How can a company determine ways to add value to a product for consumers?

_____

_____

_____

_____

REVIEW

APPLY WHAT YOU LEARNED

16. Why is the price of a product important to both consumers and businesses?

_____

_____

_____

_____

17. Why should a company be careful of changing prices quickly?

_____

_____

_____

_____

18. What are some examples of the uses of trade credit?

_____

_____

_____

_____

19. Why would a business want to develop its own credit plan rather than use a plan operated by a bank or another finance company?

_____

_____

_____

_____

20. What can a company do to move from price competition to non-price competition?

_____

_____

_____

_____

21. How can an advertisement increase the value of a product?

_____

_____

_____

_____

MAKE CONNECTIONS

22. GOVERNMENT Specific taxes collected by the federal, state, and local governments can affect the demand for certain products and services. For example, a very high tax is placed on products such as cigarettes and alcohol, while most states do not currently tax products sold on the Internet. Many local governments impose high taxes on hotels, rental cars, and restaurant meals. Gather information on tax policies of the federal government or your state's government that might influence demand for products. Write a one-page report on your findings in which you provide examples of taxes and state your opinion about the use of those types of taxes.

_____

_____

_____

_____

23. TECHNOLOGY Many Internet sites have been developed that allow consumers to quickly compare prices of products. Search the Internet to find examples of those sites. Study them to determine the information that is provided to the consumer in addition to the price of the product. Using a spreadsheet format, develop a chart that compares the sites. Develop a rating system and rate each site in terms of its value in helping customers make effective purchase decisions.

_____

_____

_____

_____

24. BUSINESS MANAGEMENT Work with a team of students to complete this exercise. Your team is responsible for developing credit policies for a home electronics store. Prepare four specific policy statements for the business that describes how credit will be extended and to whom it will be offered. Now prepare a one-page credit application to collect information from consumers that will help you decide whether they are a good candidate for credit. Present your policy statements and credit applications in class. Discuss the similarities and differences among the teams. Compare your policies and application with other teams' policies and credit applications.

25. RESEARCH Use the Internet or your local newspaper to find advertisements from three businesses that offer consumer credit. Make a list of the credit terms, interest rates, and any restrictions on the availability of credit. Determine how effectively the company explains its credit policies and terms. List any questions you would need to have answered in order to understand the company's procedures. Compare your results with that of other students. Discuss recommendations you would make to businesses to make credit more understandable to consumers.

PROMOTION

LESSONS

6.1 PROMOTION AND ADVERTISING

6.2 PERSONAL SELLING

6.3 SALES PROMOTION, PUBLICITY, INTERNET

The Chapter 6 video for this module introduces the concepts in this chapter.

PROJECT
Develop Effective Promotion

PROJECT OBJECTIVES

- Identify the role of promotion and advertising in marketing
- Discuss the effective use of personal selling
- Describe ways to improve the effectiveness of promotion

GETTING STARTED

Read through the Project Process below. Make a list of materials and information you will need. Decide how you will get the needed materials or information.

- Your class has decided to produce and sell an Alumni Album for your school. It will contain names, photos, and brief biographies of graduates, a history of the school with accompanying photos, and advertising from local businesses.
- Your team is responsible for planning promotion for the Alumni Album.

PROJECT PROCESS

Part 1 LESSON 6.1 Identify and briefly describe at least five ways the Alumni Album could be promoted for sale to graduates and their families. List the advantages and disadvantages of each. Use a computer graphics program to develop one advertisement that could be placed in a newspaper, in a magazine, or on a flyer to promote the album.

Part 2 LESSON 6.2 You are a part of a sales team that will contact business people to sell advertisements in the Alumni Album. Develop a one-page feature/benefit analysis that identifies the reasons businesses will want to advertise in the Album. Join with another student to prepare and present a sales presentation role-play to a local businessperson.

Part 3 LESSON 6.3 Using Web-design or word-processing software, develop three Internet advertisements of varying sizes and forms to promote the Alumni Album. Identify five web sites that you think would be effective locations to place the Internet advertisements. Determine ways to get publicity. Justify your choices.

Project Wrap-up As a class, discuss how decisions made about each of the other mix elements for the Alumni Album affects promotional planning. Identify ways you could determine if the promotion was effective.

LESSON 6.1
PROMOTION AND ADVERTISING

DISCUSS the role of promotion in marketing

IDENTIFY ways to use advertising effectively

THE ROLE OF PROMOTION IN MARKETING

Promotion of products in the United States is everywhere. Consumers are exposed to thousands of promotional messages each day from newspapers, radio, billboards, and even advertisements mounted on taxis or painted on city buses. To be successful, a company's promotions must interest people in buying its products and services and help them purchase the product.

Promotion refers to the methods used and information communicated to consumers. It results in a consumer's decision to purchase and in increased customer satisfaction. One of the primary reasons a company's products fail is that customers are not aware of the product or how it will satisfy their needs. Ensuring customer satisfaction is a very important part of promotion.

ON THE $CENE

Michael travels with his family each year to their summer beach home in North Carolina. For the past three years, he and a few other friends have operated a business where they provide three-hour walking tours of the resort town where they vacation. They charge $5 for adults and $3 for children ages 5 to 12. Each summer he makes enough money for spending and a small amount of savings. Michael would like to expand the business to attract even more tourists and thinks promotion might be helpful. What recommendations would you make to Michael about when, where, and how to promote his business?

Each of the other elements of the marketing mix are important to effective promotion. Consumers need to know the product is available. They also must know where they can purchase it. They must be able to easily recognize the uses and the unique features of the product and be able to compare differences among brands. They will want to know the cost of the product and be able to determine if it is a good value in satisfying their needs.

MODEL OF EFFECTIVE COMMUNICATION

Effective promotion is based on effective communication. Communication is a two-way process between a sender, the person or organization providing the information, and the receiver, one or more people with whom the sender wants to communicate. Receivers can send feedback to the sender indicating whether they understand the message or not, ask questions, or provide additional information. A basic communication model is shown below.

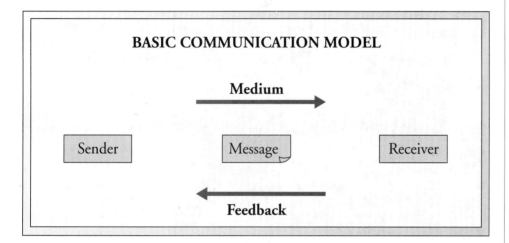

BASIC COMMUNICATION MODEL

Medium

Sender — Message — Receiver

Feedback

In promotion, the company communicating with consumers is the sender. The information in the promotion is the message. The method of promotion—advertising, personal selling, sales promotion, publicity—determines the communication medium. The prospective customer is the receiver. Feedback from the receiver will help the sender determine whether the promotion was successful and whether additional promotion and communication is needed.

ROLES OF PROMOTION

Promotion has three possible roles in marketing. It can inform, persuade, or remind. The first role of promotion is to *inform*. Customers need to be aware of a product, its features, and marketing mix elements. They must be able to identify what needs the product will satisfy.

Persuasion encourages a customer to take a specific action such as visit a store, request additional information, or purchase a product. Persuasion is an important promotion task as customers compare brands to determine those that they believe are the best value or provide the greatest satisfaction.

Finally, promotion can *remind* customers who have purchased a product about the satisfaction they received and encourage them to continue to purchase the product. Satisfied customers are important to businesses. They should not be ignored when planning promotion.

COMMUNICATION METHODS IN PROMOTION

Companies can communicate with consumers in many ways. New and creative forms of communication and promotion are regularly developed by businesses. The common forms of promotion that businesses use to communicate with customers are advertising, personal selling, sales promotion, and publicity. Media frequently used for promotion are television, newspapers, magazines, radio, direct mail, outdoor advertising, and the Internet. In addition, companies can communicate through sales letters, telephone, and face-to-face meetings with consumers.

Depending on its communications goal, a company may choose to use either personal or mass communication. **Personal communication** involves a very small number of people in direct two-way information exchange. With personal communication, the people involved in the information exchange have the ability to interact with each other. Personal selling is an example of personal communication. Customers can ask the salesperson questions and get specific information related to their needs. Personal selling is an effective way to communicate, but it also is very expensive.

Mass communication involves communicating with a large number of people at the same time with limited or no interaction. Most advertising is an example of mass communication. With this type of communication, companies do not receive feedback. It also is more general than personal communications. However, because so many people can be reached with the same message, it is more efficient.

CHECKPOINT

Name four common forms of promotion.

_____

_____

ADVERTISING AS A PROMOTIONAL TOOL

Television, radio, newspapers, magazines, direct mail, Internet—there are so many choices of ways to advertise. Each has its strengths and weaknesses and differing costs. Advertising is the most frequently used type of promotion. **Advertising** is any paid form of communication sent through a mass medium by an organization that delivers a message to many people at the same time.

Because advertising messages are designed to appeal to many people, they can be rather impersonal. A company's advertising message appears in mass media such as television and newspapers. It must compete with many other advertisements and messages also appearing in the medium. To obtain and hold the attention and interest of consumers, advertising must be unique and creative.

Organizations spend more money each year in the U.S. on advertising than on any other type of promotion. While the average business spends less than 2 percent of total sales annually on advertising, some businesses spend 20 percent or more. Companies selling products such as beverages, cosmetics, and electronics depend on advertising. They spend a significant amount of money throughout the year to keep their brand names in front of consumers.

TYPES OF ADVERTISING

Businesses use both organizational and product advertising. **Organizational advertising** promotes the company and its image rather than any specific product. **Product advertising** is designed to sell a specific product or service. When McDonald's promotes its family image it is using organizational advertising. If the company encourages customers to purchase a specific product such as a Big Mac or a Quarter Pounder, it is using product advertising.

FORMATS OF ADVERTISEMENTS

Several common formats of advertisements are available to meet the specific communications needs of businesses. The formats represent how the company is attempting to influence consumers to purchase their products.

Slice of Life These advertisements show people using the product in an everyday setting. The people in the advertisement should look and act like the target market the company has selected.

WORKSHOP

Obtain copies of five newspaper or magazine ads. For each ad, identify the format being used. Share your ads with other students and discuss the effectiveness of each based on the theme used.

Musical Musical advertisements feature a song, jingle, or popular entertainer and attempt to establish a memorable connection between the product and the music. Hot music groups or nostalgic songs may elicit positive images for consumers.

Technical or Scientific Information Some consumers want specific information about the product, its construction, use, or durability. Advertisements featuring technical information presented by a scientist, engineer, or other expert are designed to meet that communication objective.

Fantasy Fantasy ads create an ideal vision for the consumer and connect that vision to the use of the product. This format is frequently used to sell perfume, vacations, or expensive automobiles.

Testimonial Somewhat like the technical advertisements, testimonials provide endorsements about the use of the product. Entertainers, athletes, and other celebrities often provide the testimonial. Other advertisements feature the testimonials of ordinary people who represent the target market for the product.

Mood or Image These advertisements are designed to elicit emotions from the consumer making them happy, nostalgic, or excited. Companies that sell greeting cards, film for cameras, flowers, and long-distance telephone service often try to appeal to emotions connected with the use of their products.

BUSINESS MATH CONNECTION

In order to compare the costs of various media, the cost of advertising often is expressed as cost per thousand (CPM) people reached. For example, a national magazine may have 800,000 subscribers and sell an additional 225,000 individual copies each edition. If a full-page advertisement costs $125,000, what would be the CPM for the ad?

SOLUTION

Number of subscribers	+	Number of individual copies	=	Total number of customers
800,000	+	225,000	=	1,025,000

Cost of advertising ÷ (Total number of customers ÷ 1,000) = CPM
$125,000 ÷ (1,025,000 ÷ 1,000) = $125,000 ÷ 1,025 = $121.95

Character Some companies create a fictitious character to represent their product or service. The Keebler Elves produce cookies and other snacks in their tree. Smokey the Bear asks you to prevent forest fires. Popular characters from movies and cartoons are featured in advertisements to call attention to a company's product.

DEVELOP AN ADVERTISING PLAN

Companies will place advertising in several media. They will run it for weeks and months to achieve the objectives they have set. In order to coordinate the advertising activities and to make sure the desired results are achieved, companies prepare an advertising plan. The following steps are followed in creating an advertising plan.

1. *Set Objectives* Objectives are the desired results to be accomplished. Advertising objectives should support the marketing plan and identify the message to be communicated, the target market, the result expected, and the time frame.

2. *Determine the Budget* Because advertising is expensive, the company must decide how much money it can devote to promoting the product. Advertising budgets usually are based on a percentage of expected sales or by determining the amount competitors are expected to spend. The budget must be spread across the activities to be completed and the media that will be used.

3. *Develop a Theme* A consistent message should be communicated to consumers in all of the advertisements. A theme is one idea, appeal, or benefit that will be the focus of the advertising plan. You can probably identify memorable advertising themes that have been successfully used.

4. *Select the Media* Usually companies use several media for their advertising. Media are selected based on their appeal to the target market, the ability to communicate the message, costs to prepare and run the advertisements, and the time required to prepare the ads. Media frequently used for advertising and promotion are television, newspapers, magazines, radio, direct mail, outdoor advertising, and the Internet.

5. *Create the Advertisements* This is the creative process that you often think of as the work of advertisers. Very different procedures are needed to create effective advertisements for newspapers, magazines, radio, television or outdoor advertisements.

6. *Schedule the Advertisements* A specific schedule of when each advertisement will appear in the media must be developed. The ads should appear at the time the business wants customers to buy the product. If a sale is scheduled in a store and the advertisement appears a week late, the objective will not be achieved.

7. *Evaluate Advertising Effectiveness* A company will want to know if the advertising plan achieved its objectives.

- Did customers see the ad in the media?

- Did they understand the message?

- Did their opinion of the product change as a result?

The company usually will track the sale of the products before and after the advertising appears to see if the ads influenced customer actions.

CHECKPOINT

List the steps in developing an advertising plan.

_____

_____

THINK CRITICALLY

1. How can promotion increase or decrease customer satisfaction?

_____

_____

_____

_____

2. Why is feedback important when delivering promotional messages to customers?

_____

_____

_____

_____

3. Why would companies want to spend money for organizational advertising rather than product advertising?

_____

_____

_____

_____

_____

4. Why is it important to establish a budget when developing an advertising plan?

_____

_____

_____

_____

MAKE CONNECTIONS

5. **COMMUNICATION** Identify five different advertisements, each of which uses a different medium for delivering the message to the consumer. For each advertisement, identify each part of the communications model—sender, receiver, message, medium, method of feedback. Use a word-processing or graphics program to illustrate the communication model for each of the five advertisements.

6. **DECISION MAKING** Work in groups. Each group will act as an advertising planning group. The task is to promote marketing as a career choice and encourage students in your school to enroll in marketing classes. Each group has a budget of $1,000. The advertising will run for one month before students register for classes. Prepare a two-page advertising plan for the task. Present your plan to the other students in your class. Compare the plans and discuss their similarities and differences.

LESSON 6.2
PERSONAL SELLING

GOALS

DISCUSS the advantages and disadvantages of personal selling

IDENTIFY the steps in the selling process

THE NEED FOR PERSONAL SELLING

All promotional methods involve communication with customers. Much of the promotion is directed at large groups of customers. This communication typically is general because it is designed to meet the needs of many people. Consumers may not receive the information they need for specific purchases they wish to make. Unless customers are willing to gather a great deal of information on their own and determine how a company's products will meet their needs, mass communication by itself may not be effective.

ON THE $CENE

Ramona is a member of a sales team that works with large business clients to sell computer systems. She spends about one-third of her time working with engineers, accountants, and technicians planning the right system for each customer. She does a great deal of research to learn about the customers' business and changes in its industry. She meets regularly with several people in the business who can help identify the technology needs. She carefully prepares reports and plans to outline customer solutions. She often spends several months of work with one company before the plan is presented, a contract is negotiated, and a sale is made. The final system may have a price of more than a million dollars. Ramona must make sure it will meet the customer needs and that her company can make a profit on the sale. Does Ramona's work fit your perception of a salesperson? Why or why not?

Personal selling is direct, individualized communication with one or a very few customers with the goal of assessing and meeting their needs with appropriate products and services. Direct communication means the salesperson can meet and talk with the customer. Individualized communication means the salesperson can provide specific information that responds to the unique needs of the customer. As a result of using direct communication, the salesperson is able to obtain immediate feedback from the customer and respond to any questions and concerns that are expressed. The salesperson also can provide additional information needed to help the customer make the best decision.

ADVANTAGES OF PERSONAL SELLING

There are several advantages of personal selling over advertising. Most forms of advertising allow only a limited amount of information to be communicated. A salesperson spends more time with a customer and so can offer more detail. Advertisements are necessarily more general to appeal to larger numbers of customers. Personal selling is individualized and so can be very specific. Advertising is frequently one-way communication. It is difficult for the business to determine if the customer understands the information. Also consumers cannot ask questions or ask for more information in most advertising. Customer feedback is an important part of personal selling.

DISADVANTAGES OF PERSONAL SELLING

The disadvantages of personal selling include the high cost and amount of time needed to communicate with each customer. Each salesperson is responsible for contacting customers and presenting the information so the company has less control over communications. Selling is a complex and difficult job. It requires a high level of knowledge, energy, and training. It may not be easy for companies to hire and keep effective salespeople.

USES OF PERSONAL SELLING

Personal selling is used by companies that have high priced, complex, and technical products. It is often used in business-to-business marketing or in selling expensive consumer products such as houses, automobiles, expensive clothing and jewelry, and higher priced home products and electronic equipment. Effective salespeople are usually among some of the highest paid employees of a business. To justify the cost of personal selling, the promotional task must be important and the potential profit to the business high.

CHECKPOINT

What are advantages and disadvantages of personal selling to a business?

_____

_____

_____

THE PERSONAL SELLING PROCESS

Personal selling is promotion through direct, personal contact with a customer. The salesperson usually makes direct contact with the customer through a face-to-face meeting. There are many types of customers, and a salesperson must be able to adjust to each. Some customers know exactly what they want, while others are in the early stages of decision-making. Salespeople must understand each customer and then follow a set of steps to complete the selling process.

STUDY THE WANTS OF CUSTOMERS

Buying motives are the reasons people buy. Individuals are motivated to buy for different reasons. To be successful, the salesperson must determine a particular customer's buying motive and then tailor the sales presentation to appeal to it.

In many cases, the salesperson can appeal to more than one buying motive. For instance, an automobile salesperson may emphasize the roominess and safety features of a van to a family. The same salesperson selling the van to a businessperson may show how the seats can be removed quickly to be able to load and haul equipment. Both customers may be interested in the economy and low-cost maintenance of the van. Providing customer satisfaction through a sale is the ultimate goal of a salesperson. This does not require high-pressure selling. It requires intelligent customer-oriented selling.

TECH TALK

A DIFFICULT SALE Can you sell computers and Internet software in the poorest rural towns of Costa Rica or Senegal? That would seem impossible for even the best salesperson. But Hewlett Packard is doing just that, in a unique way. A large durable shipping container with screens for windows and doors sits in the middle of the village connected to the outside world by a satellite dish mounted on the roof. Inside are six PCs, a scanner, and a television. Local citizens line up outside to check e-mail, to use the Internet to obtain agricultural and health information, and to watch training videos on the television. Hewlett Packard salespeople work with the countries' government and foundations that pay for the information centers. Hewlett Packard believes even though it is a small sale, if it is the first to establish technology in the towns, it will have an advantage in those countries as their economies grow.

THINK CRITICALLY Why do salespeople work with governments and foundations rather than the local citizens? What needs of the local citizens is being satisfied with the products? What needs of the government and foundations that pay for the equipment are being satisfied?

PRESENT AND DEMONSTRATE THE PRODUCT

Customers are interested in what the product will do for them and how they can use it. Salespeople must have a thorough knowledge of the product so that they can provide accurate information and answer questions. For example, customers might ask: "What type of wood should I purchase to construct a durable deck on my home?" "Can this fabric be laundered, or do I have to have it dry cleaned?" "Why is this model of television priced $200 higher than the competing brand?"

Different customers value different types of information about the same product. Salespeople should study the products they sell as well as the competition's products so that they can be prepared to answer any questions customers might ask. In addition to giving customers information, salespeople should be able to demonstrate the use of the product so that customers can determine whether or not the product will meet their needs. The salesperson can focus the customer's attention on the product while explaining its features and benefits.

ANSWER CUSTOMER QUESTIONS

A customer usually has many questions during the salesperson's presentation. The salesperson should not be concerned by the questions but should view them as an opportunity to better understand the customer's needs and help to make the best decision. Questions may represent real concerns or may be an effort to avoid making a purchase decision. It is difficult to try to second-guess a customer to determine if the question is real or not. It is best for the salesperson to listen carefully and help the customer make the best decision.

CLOSE THE SALE

For many salespeople, the most difficult part of the selling process is asking the customer to buy. If the salesperson has involved the customer in the sales presentation and has listened carefully to the customer's needs, the customer's interest in buying should be clear. Effective salespeople give the customer the opportunity to buy several times during the sales presentation by asking for a decision on a specific model, color, price, or type of payment. If the customer continues to ask questions, the salesperson will answer them and continue the discussion until the customer appears satisfied. Then the salesperson will attempt to close the sale again. Salespeople should work with customers until it is clear they do not want the product or until the sale is made.

FOLLOW UP

The selling process is not complete just because the customer agrees to purchase a product. Remember that effective marketing results in satisfying exchanges between a business and a customer. Therefore, selling is successful only when the customer is satisfied. After the sale, the salespeople should check with the customer to be sure the order is correct, the customer knows how to use the product, and that it meets the customer's needs. If the customer has problems with the product, the salesperson should correct them immediately. If the customer is satisfied, the salesperson's follow-up contact will remind the customer where the product was purchased, so that the customer may choose to buy from the same business again.

WORKSHOP

Work with another student. Select a product. Then prepare and present a role play of a salesperson making a successful sales presentation to a customer. Present the role play to the class.

CHECKPOINT

What are the steps in the selling process?

_____

_____

THINK CRITICALLY

1. Why is it important for salespeople to have a good understanding of customers?

_____

_____

_____

_____

2. Why are professional salespeople often among the highest paid employees in an organization?

_____

_____

_____

_____

3. What are some ways that salespeople can determine the needs and buying motives of customers?

_____

_____

_____

_____

4. How can follow-up activities of salespeople result in higher sales for the company?

_____

_____

_____

_____

MAKE CONNECTIONS

5. **TECHNOLOGY** List each of the steps in the selling process on a sheet of paper or in a word-processing document. For each step, identify one way that technology can be used to aid a salesperson to complete each step. Search the Internet to see if you can identify an example of computer hardware and software that are promoted as tools to assist salespeople with the selling and sales management process. Print information on the products you locate and share the information with other students.

6. **RESEARCH** Salespeople have the responsibility to gather information about the products they represent as well as competitor's products so they can provide customers with complete and accurate information. Select one of the following products—automobile, laptop computer, high definition television—or a product your teacher assigns. Use the Internet, magazines, and other resources to research at least two comparable brands of the product selected. Prepare a written outline of product features that compares similarities and differences of the two brands.

LESSON 6.3
SALES PROMOTION, PUBLICITY, INTERNET

GOALS

IDENTIFY uses of sales promotion and publicity

EXPLAIN how the Internet is used for promotion

SALES PROMOTION AND PUBLICITY

Advertising and personal selling are the primary methods of promotion used by businesses. There are many other ways for companies to communicate with prospective and current customers as well. Important communication goals are to make the company and its products memorable in the minds of consumers and to build a positive image for the company. Sales promotion and publicity are important promotional tools used to accomplish those goals.

ON THE $CENE

A new children's movie is about to be released featuring a cartoon character. Suddenly the stores and other businesses are filled with products that feature the character. Parents can buy lunch boxes and backpacks and all types of clothing with the image and name of the character. New games are introduced and children are encouraged to send an e-mail to receive a gift and set of coupons to be used at businesses that are part of the promotion. What advantages do companies hope to obtain when they become a part of promotional campaigns tied to movies? Do you believe these types of promotional campaigns are effective? Why or why not?

USES OF SALES PROMOTION

Sales promotion is the use of activities or materials that offer customers a direct incentive to buy a product or service. Examples of sales promotions are coupons, games or contests, free samples, and rebates.

Coupons are an effective method of increasing sales of a product for a short time. They are frequently used to introduce a new product or to maintain and increase a company's share of the market for established brands. Coupons usually appear in newspaper and magazine advertisements. They also are distributed by direct mail and the Internet.

When producers are introducing a new product, they may distribute samples through the mail. The purpose of this activity is to familiarize people with the products to create a demand for them in local businesses. Coupons often accompany the samples to encourage the consumer to go to a local store and buy the product.

Manufacturers often cooperate with wholesalers and retailers by providing promotional materials. Promotional materials include window displays, layouts and illustrations for newspaper ads, direct-mail inserts, display materials, and sales presentation aids. Some of these promotional materials are commonly furnished without cost or at a low price. Companies may offer consumer demonstrations in stores. For example, demonstrators may cook and distribute samples of a new food product in the store. This practice usually helps the retailers sell the new product so the retailer gives the brand location or pricing preferences.

An effective type of sales promotion is giving items to consumers that promote the company or product. A home repair service may give a calendar or refrigerator magnet to a customer as a reminder to call the next time the service is needed. A dentist may provide a small toothbrush and tube of toothpaste to a child as a reminder of the importance of good dental care.

HOW TO MARKET A WASHING MACHINE

U.S. companies have never had success selling home appliances in India. To compete in the market for washing machines there, Whirlpool developed a full marketing campaign for its White Magic machine. Because keeping clothes from discoloring from local water in rural India is a problem, Whirlpool emphasized that the White Magic machine is especially good at washing white clothes. The marketing campaign features an advertisement showing a young girl winning a local beauty contest with a dress that is much whiter than the other contestants' dresses. Her mother, of course, used a White Magic machine. Whirlpool gives retailers higher incentives to stock and promote the machines. The company uses a network of local contractors selected because they speak one of the 18 native languages of the country. They deliver the machines using trucks or even oxcarts and install them in the buyer's home. They collect payment when they are finished.

THINK CRITICALLY From the information, why do you think the U.S. companies have not been successful in this market? Why is the advertising message an important part of marketing the washing machines?

Many consumer products are promoted using t-shirts or other apparel items that include the company's name and logo. Fast-food restaurants provide low-cost or inexpensive toys for children as an incentive for parents to visit regularly.

MANAGE PUBLICITY

An often-overlooked form of promotion that can have both positive and negative effects on a company is publicity. **Publicity** is information communicated through a mass medium that is not paid for or controlled by the company. Publicity is usually in the form of a news story carried in a newspaper or magazine or featured on television or radio. The news story may be prepared by a writer or reporter hired by the medium. It may feature positive or negative information. If a company is

A new promotional tool is "buzz" marketing. Companies identify and recruit trendsetters and give them special product information most people haven't yet heard. Then they rely on those people to spread the word to their friends through casual conversations, telephone calls, and Internet chat groups. It works well if the product is new and intriguing. What are the products that are currently being "buzzed" by groups with which you are familiar?

introducing an innovative product, it will often get positive publicity. On the other hand, if a consumer is injured using a product, the company will get negative publicity.

While publicity is not paid for or controlled by the company, most businesses work hard to get the media to include positive publicity about the company and its products. Large companies often have departments with people whose responsibility it is to prepare press releases, contact media representatives, and follow up on stories that appear in the media. If the business anticipates a problem, those people will be available to discuss the situation and provide answers on how the company will respond.

Positive publicity is important to a business. People are more likely to believe information that is not a part of an advertisement. The image of a company is enhanced when it is recognized in the media for supporting a community activity or making a contribution to charity.

The disadvantage of publicity is that the business cannot directly control the information that will appear in the media. Negative stories on a company, its products, or operations can have an impact on customer perceptions and sales.

CHECKPOINT

Define sales promotion and publicity.

_____

_____

_____

INTERNET PROMOTION

The Internet has become an important way to provide information about the company and its products to customers. As customers try to locate specific products and businesses, they are increasingly turning to the Internet. By using the Internet, a customer can often obtain product descriptions, find out the days and hours a business is open, and even print a map showing the location of the business. Today if a business has not posted information about its business, location, and products and services on the Internet, it is likely to miss some customers.

You have probably noticed when you go online that the Internet is filled with advertisements. Because space on a Web page is limited, companies compete for the attention of Internet users. They try to place their advertisements on pages that prospective customers are most likely to visit. They also use creative advertising designs. Varied sizes, colors, and placements of

advertisements encourage Internet users to stop and read the company's information. Advertisements now include moving text and graphics and links to more detailed information.

A recent innovation in Internet advertising is the "pop-up" advertisement. Companies have developed agreements with Internet service providers, browsers, and web sites that consumers frequently visit. When that web site is visited, an advertisement for the company's product pops up on the consumer's computer screen. While it may be an annoyance to some users, companies have found that the pop-up advertisements result in ten times more customer inquiries than other forms of Internet ads.

CHECKPOINT

How can the Internet be used for promotion?

_____

_____

THINK CRITICALLY

1. Why are sales promotion and publicity considered forms of promotion?

_____

_____

_____

_____

2. How can a business attempt to increase positive publicity and reduce negative publicity?

_____

_____

_____

_____

3. Why are people willing to pay money to purchase and wear apparel that promotes a company's brand name?

_____

_____

_____

_____

_____

4. Why has the Internet become such an important promotional medium even though it accounts for a very small percentage of consumer purchases?

_____

_____

_____

_____

_____

MAKE CONNECTIONS

5. JOURNALISM Search your local newspaper for examples of publicity about businesses and products. Make a photocopy of each article. Write a half-page report on each one that identifies the company and product, the purpose of the article, and whether the publicity is positive or negative for the company. Share your articles with other class members and discuss what each company should do as a result of the publicity.

6. COMMUNICATION Visit businesses in your community to identify methods of sales promotion they use. If possible, collect examples of the sales promotion tools, such as coupons, calendars, pencils, key chains, etc. Work with other students to create a display of the sales promotion tools you identified. Present your displays in class. Review all of the items in the display and discuss the purpose of each item and whether you think it is an effective communication tool for the business.

CHAPTER SUMMARY

LESSON 6.1 Promotion and Advertising

A. To be successful, a company's promotion must interest people in buying.

B. Advertising must be unique and creative to obtain and hold the attention and interest of consumers.

LESSON 6.2 Personal Selling

A. Salespeople are able to obtain immediate feedback from the customer, respond to their questions and concerns, and provide additional information needed to help the customer make the best decision.

B. Salespeople must be able to adjust to many different types of customers. Some customers know exactly what they want, while others do not.

LESSON 6.3 Sales Promotion, Publicity, Internet

A. Important communication goals are to make the company and its products memorable and to build a positive image for the company.

B. Consumers are exposed to thousands of promotions each day from many different sources, including the Internet.

VOCABULARY BUILDER

Choose the term that best fits the definition. Write the letter of the answer in the space provided. Some terms may not be used.

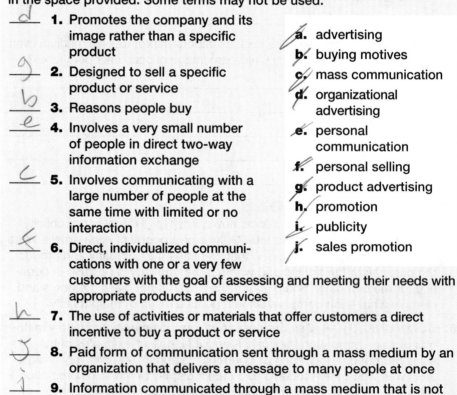

___d___ **1.** Promotes the company and its image rather than a specific product

___g___ **2.** Designed to sell a specific product or service

___b___ **3.** Reasons people buy

___e___ **4.** Involves a very small number of people in direct two-way information exchange

___c___ **5.** Involves communicating with a large number of people at the same time with limited or no interaction

___f___ **6.** Direct, individualized communications with one or a very few customers with the goal of assessing and meeting their needs with appropriate products and services

___h___ **7.** The use of activities or materials that offer customers a direct incentive to buy a product or service

___j___ **8.** Paid form of communication sent through a mass medium by an organization that delivers a message to many people at once

___i___ **9.** Information communicated through a mass medium that is not paid for or controlled by the company

___a___ **10.** The methods used and information communicated to consumers resulting in a purchase decision and customer satisfaction

a. advertising

b. buying motives

c. mass communication

d. organizational advertising

e. personal communication

f. personal selling

g. product advertising

h. promotion

i. publicity

j. sales promotion

REVIEW CONCEPTS

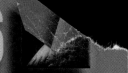

POINT YOUR BROWSER

b2000.swep.com

11. What determines if a company's promotion is successful or not?

The rate that people buy the product being advertised determines the success.

12. What are the parts of an effective communication model?

medium

sender → message → receiver

feedback

13. How much does the average company spend on advertising?

The average amount of money a company spends on advertising is 10 million

14. Why is mass communication by itself usually not effective?

because it is a much broader method of communication

15. What types of companies are likely to use personal selling?

Smaller companies are more likely to use personal selling, such as a jewelry store.

16. What are two important communication goals for which publicity and sales promotion are used?

To get your message out there and prove that your product is better than the competitors.

APPLY WHAT YOU LEARNED

17. Why is it difficult for companies to determine how much to spend on advertising and if their advertising investments are effective?

because you don't want to under-budget or over-budget.

18. When would a company choose to use mass communication rather than personal communication?

When you are going to advertise on a much larger scale and want to appeal to a large mass of people.

19. What is the advantage of using a team of people to sell complex and expensive products rather than relying on one salesperson to work with a customer?

It is much easier to work with a team so you can divvy up the responsibilities.

20. Why do inexperienced salespeople often have difficulty closing the sale?

because you have to persuade the customer in every aspect.

21. What are the differences between advertising and publicity?

Advertising is the ads on tv and stuff. Publicity is just word of mouth.

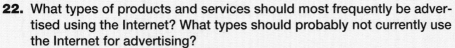
22. What types of products and services should most frequently be advertised using the Internet? What types should probably not currently use the Internet for advertising?

Stuff that you can buy in bulk should be advertised on the internet

MAKE CONNECTIONS

23. PSYCHOLOGY Effective promotion appeals to the buying motives of customers. Use newspapers, magazines, television, and the Internet to identify five advertisements. For each advertisement, identify the target market to which the advertisement is appealing, the buying motive that seems to be the focus of the advertising message, and the features of the product that are designed to appeal to the buying motive identified.

24. INTERNATIONAL BUSINESS Identify a product manufactured in the United States that could be sold in another country. Use resources from your library and the Internet to gather information about a country that you think would be a good market for the product. Prepare a two-page report that could be used by salespeople and advertising specialists to help them understand consumers in the country so that the company's promotion will be effective.

25. BUSINESS MANAGEMENT Work with a team of students to develop a promotional plan for a product the team selects. Identify the primary target market for the product. Develop two advertisements for the product and identify the media in which the advertisements will run. Design two methods of sales promotion for the product. Prepare an information sheet about the product that would be helpful for a salesperson to understand the product. Write a news release to send to media to generate publicity for the product. Present your team's promotion plan in class.

26. RESEARCH Use the Internet or business magazines to identify the following information.

  A. The 10 companies who spent the most on advertising in a recent year and the amount each company spent on advertising.
  B. The amount of money spent in each of the major advertising media (newspaper, television, magazines, etc.) in a recent year.
  C. Summarize your findings using a spreadsheet format.

GLOSSARY

A

Advertising any paid form of communication sent through a mass medium by an organization that delivers a message to many people at the same time (p. 135)

B

Basic product the physical product in its simplest form (p. 64)

Brand a name, symbol, word, or design that identifies a product, service, or company (p. 65)

Bricks and mortar a business that completes most of its business activities in traditional ways (p. 21)

Business information the type of information the business needs to collect in order to understand its strengths and weaknesses (p. 39)

Business markets the companies and organizations that purchase products for the operations of a business or the completion of a business activity (p. 50)

Buying behavior the decision processes and actions of consumers as they buy and use services and products (p. 48)

Buying motives the reasons consumers buy (p. 46)

C

Capital equipment the land buildings and major pieces of equipment that are usually the most expensive products purchased by a business (p. 52)

Channels of distribution the routes that products follow in moving from the producer to the consumer including all related activities and participating organizations (p. 89)

Component parts elements of products that a business makes that are processed partially or totally by another company (p. 52)

Consumer credit credit extended by a retail business to a consumer (p. 117)

Customer information information on prospective customers that is used to select the best target markets (p. 39)

D

Decline stage occurs when a new product is introduced that is much better or easier to use and customers switch from the old product to the new product (p. 74)

Direct distribution when producers sell directly to the consumer (p. 89)

Direct marketing the producer sells and distributes its products to consumers (p. 89)

Distribution determining the best methods and procedure to be used so customers are able to locate, obtain, and use the products and services of an organization (p. 6)

Distribution makes the product available where and when the customer wants it (p. 35)

Dot.com a business that completes most of its business activities through the Internet (p. 21)

E

E-commerce the exchange of goods, services, information, or other business through electronic means (p. 20)

Economic utility the amount of satisfaction a consumer receives from the consumption of a particular product or service (p. 12)

Emotional motives reasons to purchase based on feelings (p. 46)

Enhanced product adds features and options to the basic product (p. 64)

Evaluation of alternatives consumers use information they gather to evaluate their buying choices (p. 48)

Exchange two people of an organization involved in a transaction (p. 5)

Experiments tightly controlled situations in which all important factors are the same except the one being studied (p. 43)

Exporting selling products and services to markets in other countries (p. 100)

Extended product includes additional features that are not part of the physical product but increases its usability (p. 64)

External information provides an understanding of factors outside of the organization (p. 41)

F

Features added to improve the basic product (p. 64)

Financing includes budgeting for marketing activities, obtaining the necessary financing, and providing financial assistance to customers to assist them with purchasing the organization's products and services (p. 117)

Form utility results from actual changes in the product (p. 12)

Franchising allows a service to be provided in a variety of locations while maintaining a consistent image and level of quality (p. 80)

G

Growth stage point in the product life cycle when several brands of a new product are available (p. 74)

H

Hierarchy of needs identifies five areas that guide behavior—physiological, security, social, esteem, and self-actualization (p. 46)

I

Image a unique, memorable quality of a brand (p. 65)

Importing purchasing products and services that are produced in other countries (p. 100)

Indirect distribution when distribution involves other businesses in addition to the producer (p. 89)

Inform first role of promotion (p. 133)

Information search the consumer gathers information about alternative solutions (p. 48)

Internal information information that flows through a business that is valuable for marketing (p. 40)

J

Joint venture an agreement between independent companies to participate in common business activities (p. 100)

L

Law of demand the relationship between price and purchase decisions (p. 11)

Law of supply the relationship between price and product decisions (p. 11)

Loyalty motives based on satisfying relationships (p. 47)

M

Maintenance contract a support service that will pay for repair work if the product fails to operate properly (p. 65)

Markdown reduction in price (p. 114)

Market a broad group of prospective customers that a company wants to serve (p. 33)

Marketing develops and maintains satisfying exchange relationships between business and consumers (p. 5)

Marketing concept using the needs of customers as the primary focus during the planning, production, and promotion of a product or service (p. 17)

Marketing information management obtaining, managing, and using market information to improve business decision making and the performance of marketing activities (p. 6)

Marketing information system allows the information from many sources to be collected, stored and analyzed when needed to improve new product decisions (p. 68)

Marketing mix the blending of four marketing elements—products, distributions, price, and promotion (p. 34)

Marketing research a procedure designed to identify solutions to a specific marketing problem through the use of scientific problem-solving (p. 42)

Marketing strategy a company's plan that identifies how it will use marketing to achieve its goals (p. 33)

Markup the amount added to the cost of the goods to cover all other expenses plus a profit (p. 113)

Mass communication involves communication with a large number of people at the same time with limited or no interaction (p. 134)

Maturity stage the product has many competing brands with similar features (p. 74)

Mixed merchandise store offers products from several different categories (p. 97)

Multinational business companies that have operations in many other countries and that regularly engage in international business (p. 101)

N

Need anything you require to live (p. 45)

Non-price competition emphasizes factors other than price as the important reason for customers to buy (p. 122)

Non-profit organization organizations that have specific goals of clients that they are organized to serve and providing that service is the reason they exist. While they need an adequate budget to operate, profit is not the primary motive for their existence (p. 51)

Non-store retailing sells directly to the consumer's home rather than requiring the consumer to travel to a store (p. 97)

O

Observation collects information by recording people's actions without interacting or communicating with the participant (p. 43)

Operating equipment smaller less expensive equipment used in the operation of the business or in the production and sale of products and services (p. 52)

Organizational advertising promotes the company and its image rather than any specific product (p. 135)

P

Packaging provides protection and security for the product during distribution (p. 65)

Personal communication involves a very small number of people in a direct two-way information exchange (p. 134)

Personal selling direct, individualized communications with one or a very few customers with the goal of assessing and meeting their needs with appropriate products and services (p. 141)

Persuasion encourages a customer to take a specific action such as visit a store, request additional information, or purchase a product (p. 133)

Place utility making products and services available where the consumer wants them (p. 12)

Possession utility makes products and services more affordable (p. 13)

Post-purchase evaluation the consumer uses the purchase and decides it if met the need or solved the problem (p. 48)

Price the cost of the product or service paid by the customer (p. 111)

Price competition rivalry among businesses where the primary difference is the price offered (p. 122)

Pricing establishing and communicating the value of products and services to prospective customers (p. 111)

Problem recognition the consumer recognizes a need (p. 48)

Product anything offered to a market by the business to satisfy needs (p. 63)

Product advertising designed to sell a specific product or service (p. 135)

Product life cycles the stages of sales and profit performance through which all brands of a product progress as a result of competition (p. 73)

Product/service planning assisting in the design and development of products and services that will meet the needs or prospective customers (p. 67)

Promotion the methods used and information communicated to consumers (p. 132)

Prototype a sample of the product (p. 71)

Publicity information communicated through a mass medium that is not paid for or controlled by the company (p. 148)

Purchase decision if a suitable choice is available and affordable the consumer will make a selection and complete the purchase (p. 48)

Purchase volume the number of business customers that make up a market for a particular type of product (p. 53)

R

Rational motives reasons to buy based on facts or logic (p. 46)

Raw materials unprocessed products used as basic materials for the products to be produced (p. 52)

Retailers the final business organization in an indirect channel of distribution for consumer products (p. 96)

S

Sales promotion the use of activities or materials that offer customers a direct incentive to buy a product or service (p. 147)

Selling communicating directly with prospective customers to assess and satisfy their needs (p. 6)

Selling price price consumers are charged for a product or service (p. 113)

Service businesses activities provided directly to the customer by a business. Services cover a broad range of activities including insurance, transportation, accounting, cleaning, repair and many others (p. 51)

Services activities that do not result in the ownership of anything tangible (p. 79)

Single- or limited-line store offers products from one category of merchandising or closely related items (p. 96)

Superstore very large stores that offer consumers wide choices of products (p. 97)

Supplies products and materials consumed in the operation of a business (p. 52)

Survey a planned set of questions to which individuals or groups of people respond (p. 43)

T

Target market a smaller group or segment of a market in which customers have similar characteristics and needs (p. 33)

Test market a small representative part of the total market (p. 69)

Time utility results from making the product or service available when the customer wants it (p. 12)

Trade credit financing offered by one business to another business (p. 117)

W

Want an unfulfilled desire (p. 45)

Wholesalers companies that assist with distribution activities between businesses (p. 95)

INDEX

PHOTO CREDITS

Cover art © Eyewire.
Photo on page 143 © Corbis Digital Stock.
All other photos © PhotoDisc, Inc.